The Historic Memorial District
— OF —
DOWNTOWN INDIANAPOLIS

RUDY SCHOUTEN

Published by The History Press
Charleston, SC
www.historypress.com

Copyright © 2020 by Rudy Schouten
All rights reserved

Front cover, top: Bass Photo Co. Collection, Indiana Historical Society; *bottom left*: Bass Photo Co. Collection, Indiana Historical Society; *bottom right*: Bass Photo Co. Collection, Indiana Historical Society.

Back cover, top left: photo by Rudy Schouten, 2018; *top right*: photo by Rudy Schouten; *bottom*: photo courtesy of the Indiana War Memorials Commission.

First published 2020

Manufactured in the United States

ISBN 9781467141826

Library of Congress Control Number: 2020930468

Notice: The information in this book is true and complete to the best of our knowledge. It is offered without guarantee on the part of the author or The History Press. The author and The History Press disclaim all liability in connection with the use of this book.

All rights reserved. No part of this book may be reproduced or transmitted in any form whatsoever without prior written permission from the publisher except in the case of brief quotations embodied in critical articles and reviews.

CONTENTS

Acknowledgements 5
Introduction 7

PART I: THE FOOTPRINTS IN THE TRAIL
A Place of Distinction 11
Indianapolis: Out of the Wilderness (1780–1820) 13
The City Blueprint (1821–1889) 16

PART II: INDY'S MONUMENTS AND MEMORIALS
The Properties 23
The Mission 25

PART III: A WALK ALONG THE GRANITE AND THE LIMESTONE
Stop 1: The Soldiers and Sailors Monument 29
Stop 2: University Park 58
Stop 3: Indiana War Memorial 74
Stop 4: Veterans Memorial Plaza 100
Stop 5: American Legion Mall 112

PART IV: THE CANAL MEMORIALS
Stop 6: The USS *Indianapolis* CA35 National Memorial 135
Stop 7: The Indiana 9/11 Memorial 137
Stop 8: The Medal of Honor Memorial 139

Contents

Part V: All Welcome Places
Historic Designations   143
Gathering Places   145
Visitor Information   147
A Noble Purpose   151

Bibliography   155
About the Author   159

ACKNOWLEDGEMENTS

The objective set for *The Historic Memorial District of Downtown Indianapolis* is that it serves as a concise and interesting contribution to the telling of the city's history. If it lands anywhere in the vicinity, it would not have been possible without the excellent resources available through some of Indiana's fine civic, cultural and historical groups.

I would like to thank, in particular, Brigadier General Stewart Goodwin, executive director of the Indiana War Memorials Commission, for sharing his unique perspectives on the origins of the war memorials as well as the special challenges that come with furthering the commission's work. General Goodwin also provided welcome access to the expertise and the world of resources he has at his disposal. Ethan Wright, museum director at the Indiana War Memorial, and his staff, Chase Brazel and Jennifer Watson, went above and beyond in providing rare vintage photographs of the memorials under construction. Jason Edwardson, also on staff as tour manager at the memorial, eagerly offered up a personal tour and a few of the lesser-known secrets in the structure's architecture. And Marie Beason, executive director of the Indiana War Memorials Foundation, shared valued insight into the city's engagement with the memorial properties as well as a look into the special role played by the foundation in supporting the Memorials Commission.

But Indianapolis is full of museums and aficionados of local history willing to share from their research, their records and their vast collections touching in some way on every property described in this book. Big thanks

Acknowledgements

are in order for Nadia Kousari, visual reference coordinator at the Indiana Historical Society; Suzanne Stanis, director of heritage education and information at Indiana Landmarks; and Tiffany Benedict Browne and the capable writers and researchers who have served her mission so well over the years at HistoricIndianapolis.com.

The Historic Memorial District of Downtown Indianapolis was intended as a compact summary, but the subject of the book is anything but simple or one dimensional. The research required for presenting even a digestible version covers a lot of ground, so it has been immensely helpful to have the services of informed and enthusiastic people pointing me in the right direction.

INTRODUCTION

The most visible assets of a community, the things that give it character and personality, can also, ironically, blend humbly into the background. City monuments are like that. They are regarded for standing tirelessly in a show of great dignity, but they would not survive or serve a deeper purpose without the equally humble, endless work it takes to manage them and to draw people inside.

Here in Indianapolis, the Indiana War Memorials Commission, a state agency, manages twenty-five acres and eight properties in the heart of the city honoring Hoosier veterans and commemorating the valor and sacrifice of the United States Armed Forces. The core group of those properties consists of the Soldiers and Sailors Monument on Monument Circle and the Indiana War Memorial Plaza, an in-line stretch of parks, fountains, museums, monuments and memorials pointing the way to the north side of the city from the circle. They are the focus of this book—a look into the origins of Indy's trail of monuments, brief histories of the land on which they were built and a few morsels on what visitors will see in them with a closer look.

Providing a perspective on those three layers of the story in one piece is the goal of *The Historic Memorial District of Downtown Indianapolis*, but the approach used in writing it has a certain purpose, too. This is for anyone who has ever wondered what those monuments and memorials are all about, whether they happen to be visitors to our city or Indy locals who have walked past every one of those creations a thousand times. But it also tries not to

Introduction

do too much. If you're curious and want to know a little bit more than you do, this is a happy middle point between a handful of pamphlets and a long wade, waist deep, into the volumes at the Indiana State Museum or the Indiana Historical Society.

There are civic and personal sides to this, too. I'm one of those who have rushed past the monuments a thousand times without ever really stopping to look or think very hard about what they mean. But I know enough to understand that someone else made the kind of sacrifice it takes to make those beautiful, but ultimately unfortunate, things an idea to begin with. The least any of us can do is to make an effort, maybe more than once a year on Memorial Day or Veterans Day, to comprehend it all just a little more completely, which is to honor it. As a kid, I played on the tanks and the cannons that anchored the corners of Veterans Memorial Plaza. The tanks and the cannons are now long gone, but our monuments and memorials are among the few things on the Indy skyline that haven't changed all that much in the last fifty years. And there is, fortunately, a reason for that.

Part I

THE FOOTPRINTS IN THE TRAIL

A PLACE OF DISTINCTION

Those of us fortunate enough to live or work in Indianapolis draw a powerful sense of identity from the Mile Square, the compact heart of our city. It's the look and feel of the place, for sure, but it's not just about the fine new hotels, the great restaurants or the gleaming office towers lining the streets. Every big city has that. It's something else, and we tend not to notice that something else very often because it's just part of who we are; not unlike, for example, losing sight of the fact that we're home to the world's most famous racecourse. It takes a fresh new look every now and then to see it again, and so it is with downtown Indianapolis.

Much of what makes it unique and memorable is the harvest of granite and limestone memorials along Meridian Street. Officially, we know it as the Indiana War Memorials Historic District, a collective tribute to ordinary Hoosiers who have served our country. Those monuments remind us that thousands of men and women have done extraordinary things, which is reason enough to have the memorials there. And yet, the half-mile stretch of land they cover is only the beginning of the story, only a manifestation of a state's historic and concerted efforts to honor its heroes. It largely defines Indianapolis.

It isn't an uncommon reference in our city's literature, but it bears repeating in perhaps a different way: Greater Indianapolis has more acreage dedicated to honoring veterans than any other city in the country, and it ranks second only to Washington, D.C., in terms of the total number of memorials it has gracing the landscape. Those would be high distinctions for any community and, as intuition might suggest, a rather unlikely accomplishment for a midsized city in the Midwest. World-class monuments don't rise out of the ground without considerable resources, political clout, critical mass and a certain level of panache. So it wouldn't necessarily be a sign of civic insecurity in us to ask how they ended up in Indianapolis.

And the answer to that question begins with a look at how Indianapolis ended up where *it* is.

INDIANAPOLIS

Out of the Wilderness (1780–1820)

A logical, convenient starting point for a condensed history of Indianapolis and why it is where it is might be the day in 1780 when three hundred boatloads of white settlers floating down the Ohio River stopped near Louisville. Some of them settled there in Kentucky, some continued down the river into the Mississippi Valley and the rest turned north to help pioneer the Northwest Territory, which was officially organized seven years later.

William Henry Harrison was appointed governor of the new territory, and Vincennes was named its capital in 1800. Governor Harrison's Battle of Tippecanoe in 1811 was the territory's approach to helping settlers establish farms and homesteads quickly and safely, which also helped them turn some of their attention to the urgency of politics and government. So, the movers and the shakers went to work. In 1813, the territorial capital was moved from Vincennes to Corydon, and in 1816, Indiana was admitted as the nineteenth state.

Indiana grew at a healthy clip. A territory with fewer than 5,000 settlers in 1800—and 64,000 in 1816, the year of statehood—would balloon to a population of nearly 150,000 in 1820. The flood of new settlers and new commerce, and the evolving needs for governing the territory, led quickly to a general, although not unanimous, conclusion: perhaps the capital should be moved to a spot near the geographic center of the state, where government services and the wheels of commerce would be more accessible to all of its citizens. Placing the new capital in central Indiana would also present it with vast natural resources and ready access to the White River, seen as ideal for transporting products and raw materials throughout the new territory. It would be the key to rapid and sustained growth.

But a relocation of the capital to the center of the state would not be without major obstacles, not the least of which was the Native American population occupying the territory. After the long struggle to stay where they were, the people eventually found it prudent to come to some kind of peaceful agreement with the new settlers. In 1818, the chiefs of the Delaware, Miami and Potawatomi tribes signed the Treaty of St. Mary's (the New Purchase Treaty), relinquishing control of the land. The central third of the state was to be vacated by the resident tribes within three years, clearing the way for an orderly settlement of the region and a new capital somewhere near the center of the state.

Another obstacle was a matter of geography—and nature. The land made available by the New Purchase Treaty was still a swampy wilderness far removed from population centers in southern Indiana. Cities like Corydon and Madison fought to keep the state capital nearby, and they knew that clearing a vast wilderness so far away to build a new city would be a daunting prospect for everyone. But the state proceeded.

In 1820, Jonathan Jennings, Indiana's first governor after statehood, appointed a commission of ten men to consider locations within the New Purchase boundaries as the site for the new capital. They, of course, found the area highly uninhabitable and highly inhospitable; there were, nonetheless, a few pioneers waiting to show them around. John McCormick is credited with being the first white settler in the area when, earlier in the same year, he and his two brothers built a double cabin on the West Fork of the White River, just north of present-day Washington Street. He is also widely known to have established the settlement's first sawmill, first tavern (located conveniently inside the cabin) and first ferry service crossing White River.

George Pogue, a blacksmith from Connersville, was a neighbor in the area as well and may have actually arrived before McCormick, but Pogue vanished from the settlement within a year or two. It was widely believed that he had wandered from his cabin one day in search of some missing horses and never returned.

A commission established by the state legislature met in June of that year, convening, for lack of more stately options, in McCormick's tavern. After surveying the region, the commission identified three properties considered "most eligible and advantageous" as locations for the new state capital:

The Footprints in the Trail

Marker at the site of John McCormick's cabin along the White River, just north of Washington Street in White River State Park, 2019. *Photo by Rudy Schouten, 2019.*

William Connor's homestead near present-day Noblesville, Jacob Whetzel's farm near Waverly and the Fall Creek Settlement along the White River. William Connor had arrived in 1800 to trade with the Delaware tribe, Jacob Whetzel had migrated north from Kentucky in 1811 and the Fall Creek Settlement was part of the area first homesteaded by the likes of the Pogues and the McCormicks.

After due consideration, the commission reported back to the legislature, recommending the location near the McCormick cabin, citing three reasons: the site provided easy access to the White River, the land was flat and therefore suitable for construction and the location would be largely centered on the path of the proposed National Road. The state legislature accepted the commission's recommendations early the following year.

Picking a name for the city was the next order of business. Judge Jeremiah Sullivan of Madison suggested "Indianapolis," meaning "City of Indiana," which drew a bit of criticism, ostensibly for its shortages in the creativity department. But no other single idea placed before the legislature proved more popular. So it was agreed, and Indianapolis was incorporated on January 6, 1821. The new capital city had its name and a spot in the center of the state map. All that was left to do was build it. And that's what Governor Jennings wanted all along—a blank canvas of wilderness and the opportunity to build a new city from the ground up.

THE CITY BLUEPRINT (1821-1889)

A second commission was appointed by the legislature in 1821. Judge Christopher Harrison, commissioner for the survey of Indiana's new capital; Alexander Ralston; and Englishman Elias Pym Fordham were selected to survey and plat the city. Ralston, a native of Scotland, had worked as a surveyor in Great Britain before immigrating to the United States to assist in the mapping of Washington, D.C.

In April, Ralston suggested a "Mile Square" plan, a city grid in which most of the streets would cross at right angles, but with four diagonal avenues radiating from a central circle. It was a design similar to Pierre L'Enfant's street design for the nation's capital. Ralston's plan provided for one hundred twelve-lot blocks. There would be nine north–south streets and nine east–west streets, each ninety feet wide. The four square blocks in the middle were to be called Governor's Square. The diagonal avenues and a central three-acre circle within Governor's Square would create a formal focus on a small knoll on which the governor's residence would be built. The grid would then be balanced by statehouse and courthouse squares to the east and west, marketplaces and blocks reserved for religious purposes. Ralston's original design held up well in early development, with the exception of a modification to the overall grid pattern on the southeastern corner of town for the swampy depression along a stream known as Pogue's Run.

The summer of 1821, the first summer in the existence of Indianapolis, was a particularly hot and humid affair. The swamp-like conditions in

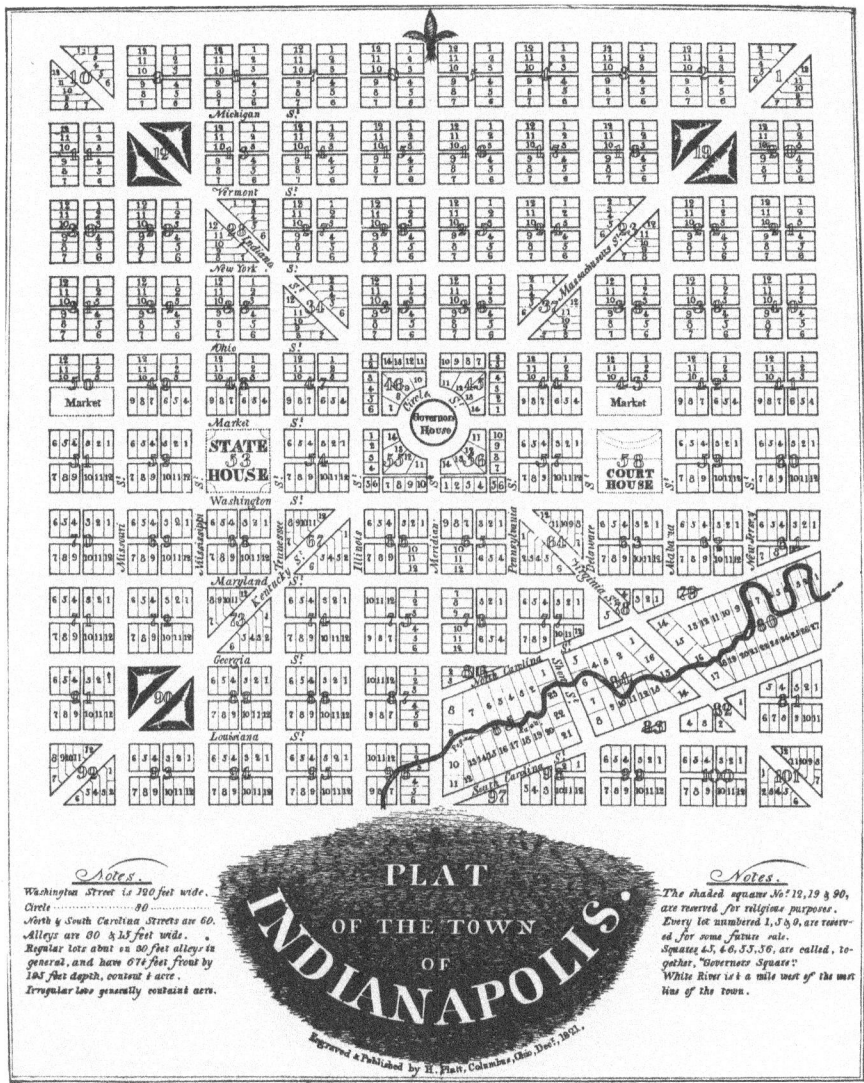

Alexander Ralston's original plat of the town of Indianapolis. *Bass Photo Co. Collection, Indiana Historical Society.*

the area and the stagnant water in Fall Creek gave rise to a bumper crop of mosquitos, sickening the early settlers with fever and other symptoms consistent with malaria. By the time the health crisis began to subside in the fall, one in every eight residents had died.

But the survivors persevered, and they capitalized on an opportunity. In October, 314 lots in Ralston's plat, to be used for the construction of homes and buildings, were sold for $35,596 in cash and promissory notes, the going rate no more than $200 to $300 per lot. As the land was cleared for dirt streets and the first permanent structures on the grid, a small patch of dense central Indiana forest was transformed into a village slowly opening to the sky. And by late 1825, Indianapolis could boast a post office, several churches, a school, a gristmill, a brickyard, two sawmills, several shops, seven taverns and a courthouse—enough civilization, officially, to bring the seat of Indiana state government up from Corydon. A new city was underway.

The early settlers had their hands full building the rough foundations for a new city. Alexander Ralston's blueprint was a good start, but there would be no progress without a few potholes in the dirt road. From the outset, the harsh conditions that killed many of the pioneers simply drove others away; some of the first lots to be sold were later forfeited, and others remained unsold for many years.

The White River was also not exactly as advertised. In February 1825, the state legislature commissioned Ralston to survey the White River and estimate the expense for "keeping it navigable." The politicians had selected the location for the capital city believing the White River would be suitable for flatboats and barges headed to the Wabash River and then on to the Ohio, but they were apparently too smitten with the beauty of the setting along the White River to evaluate, fully, its viability as a commercial waterway. Tests suggested the river wasn't really deep enough.

Ralston persisted, however, and was among the early supporters of a proposal to round out the state's commercial waterways with the development of a central canal. In 1836, the Indiana General Assembly enacted an "internal improvement bill" that included initial plans for an Indianapolis link to four hundred miles of canals through Indiana, essentially connecting the Great Lakes with the Ohio River. It would, in particular, provide an artery of commercial traffic connecting Indianapolis by water to places like Evansville, Terre Haute, Fort Wayne and Toledo, Ohio. Construction started two years later, but the state quickly ran out of money and was forced to abandon the project. Only nine miles of the Indianapolis section of the canal was completed. That part of the Central Canal was opened in 1839, but not for its intended purpose.

It would have been next to unthinkable to plan a new and respectable capital city without reasonable access to a navigable river or system of waterways, so Indianapolis found itself starting with a serious disadvantage against other, more established cities in the Midwest. But it wouldn't take long for it to uncover the beginning of an impressive Plan B. Indianapolis pivoted away from the White River and the canal miscalculations to find its own competitive advantage when it began to focus on developing a network of roads and railroads that would ultimately provide better, more efficient access to markets than the rivers or canals could.

A full, functioning city government was slow in coming for Indianapolis because the city was created, first and foremost, to be the seat of *state* government. The first town government for the city wasn't formed until 1832, more than ten years after its founding. So, nothing happened overnight, but the city was making progress in the work of becoming a vital, prosperous place to live, and city leaders and the captains of industry concentrated most urgently on matters of transportation.

The politicians tasked with picking a site for the new capital city may have missed the boat on the White River, but they weren't wrong about its position along the coming National Road. The stretch passing through the heart of Indianapolis was constructed in the 1830s, while all around it the city's street grid grew quickly beyond the boundaries of the Mile Square. The first railroad came to Indianapolis in 1847. The city's Union Depot, America's first union station, a train depot shared by all railroads entering a city, was built in 1853; and the decade of the 1850s saw a tremendous surge in the construction of new railroads and new rail services.

The era marked the first in a long line of city initiatives to distinguish itself for its elemental sense of adaptability. Indianapolis became the "Railroad City," and then, as those tracks began to stretch farther out and crisscross with more density, it became "The Crossroads of America." Over time, the image expanded with the continued development of U.S. 40, Michigan Road as a major north–south thoroughfare, additional city streets, new state highways and, eventually, the interstate highway system all coursing through Greater Indianapolis.

As additional branding opportunities presented themselves, Indianapolis would also be known, at one time or another, as "Toolmaker to the Nation" for its industrial prowess earlier in the twentieth century, the "100% American City" for its demographics representing most perfectly an American city in the Midwest, "Naptown" for the city's appeal to jazz musicians of the 1930s, the "Racing Capital of the World" for the Indianapolis Motor Speedway and the "Amateur Sports Capital of the World" for Indy's first significant forays into drawing sporting events to the city.

But no moniker for the city has been as enduring or as emblematic as the one that recalls its beginning. Indianapolis is, above all, the "Circle City," the perfect name for the home of Monument Circle, the heart of Alexander Ralston's original city plat and the spot where the Soldiers and Sailors Monument would begin to rise out of the ground in 1889. It is the foundation and the forerunner to the city's mall of memorials.

Part II

INDY'S MONUMENTS AND MEMORIALS

THE PROPERTIES

An overview of the prominent war memorials in Indianapolis starts with what we see today. The properties include the Soldiers and Sailors Monument; the Indiana War Memorial Plaza, just north of the circle between Meridian and Pennsylvania Streets; and three additional memorials lining the Indianapolis Central Canal Walk. They are all operated by the Indiana War Memorials Commission, which was established by the state legislature in 1923 to design, build and manage the newly created Indiana War Memorial Plaza. The commission itself is made up of nine commissioners, one from each of the state's congressional districts. All of them are, by statute, appointed by the governor to three-year terms, and all members must be veterans of one of the armed services.

The properties along Meridian Street, set in open landscapes designed to accent its monuments and sculptural ensembles, consists of University Park, the Indiana War Memorial, Veteran's Memorial Plaza and the American Legion Mall, which includes memorials to veterans of World War II, the Korean War and Vietnam. The plaza, now known as the Indiana War Memorials Historic District, blends with the character of other prominent buildings along Meridian Street to form a distinct collection of neoclassical structures representative of City Beautiful, an urban-planning movement that flourished in America from the 1890s to the 1920s. It is centered on the idea of merging architectural and landscape design with social needs—all in a way that encourages greater civic pride and community engagement.

The Historic Memorial District of Downtown Indianapolis

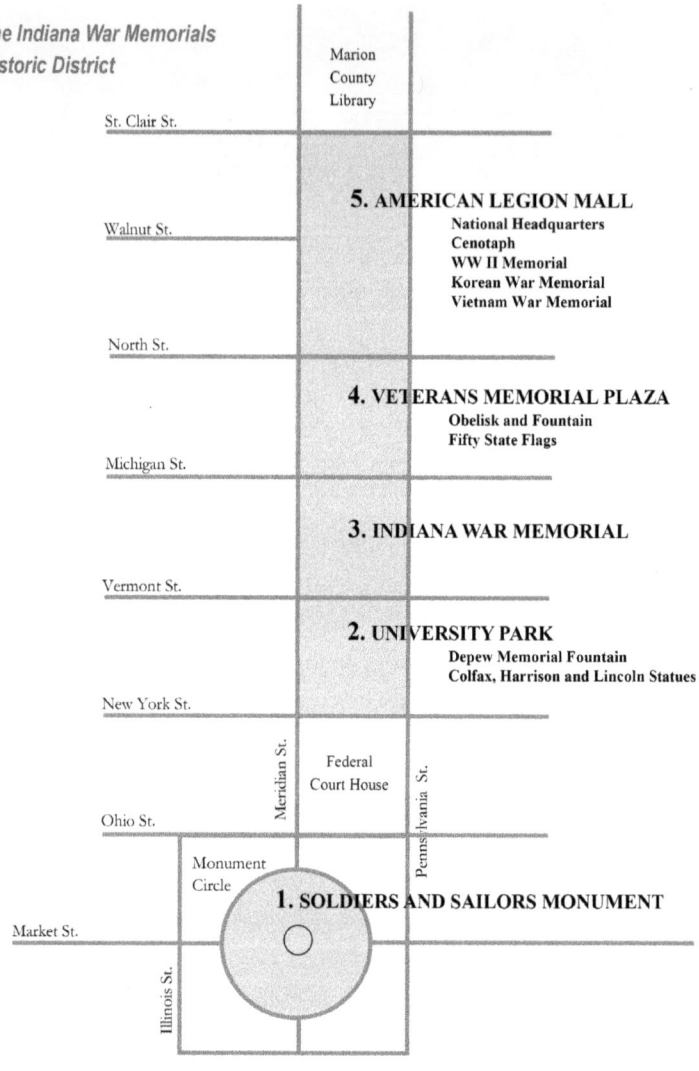

Map of Soldiers and Sailors Monument and War Memorials. *Map by Rudy Schouten.*

The memorials located along the nearby canal include the USS Indianapolis CA35 Memorial at Senate Avenue and Walnut Street on the north end of the Canal Walk; the Indiana 9/11 Memorial on the west side of the Canal Walk at West Ohio Street; and the Medal of Honor Memorial, situated along the south leg of the Canal Walk in White River State Park.

THE MISSION

All holdings of the Indiana War Memorials Commission are managed with a solemn and singular mission: "To commemorate the valor and sacrifice of the United States Armed Forces and to honor Hoosier veterans and Indiana's role in the nation's conflicts."

War memorials are no more a point of joy or celebration than are the horrors that made them necessary. But outside of making a point of enjoying our freedoms gratefully and responsibly, they are our way of remembering and saying, "Thank you." We do well, of course, to do that, and Indianapolis has done it especially well.

None of it has happened quickly or without considerable commitment. The trail of war memorials in Indianapolis, the ones described in this book, stretches from the placement of the first statue in University Park in 1887 to the dedication of the Indiana 9/11 Memorial along the canal on September 11, 2011, and it continues into 2020 with the planned addition of the Gold Star Memorial in American Legion Mall. Our statues, parks, monuments and memorials have coalesced over time into one citywide tribute to national service, but each of the properties along Meridian Street, in particular, has a purpose and a history unto itself.

Part III

A WALK ALONG THE GRANITE AND THE LIMESTONE

STOP 1
THE SOLDIERS AND SAILORS MONUMENT

THE KNOLL IN THE CITY GRID

Alexander Ralston had big plans for that little knoll in the middle of his mile-square brainchild. The three-acre circle would be the focal point of the city, so whatever was built there needed to be worthy of its lofty location, and nothing would be more fitting than building the governor's residence on the spot, just two blocks east of Indiana's new seat of state government.

The state legislature allocated $4,000 for the construction of the governor's mansion as envisioned by Ralston, and the two-story, four-room, yellow-brick structure inside Governor's Circle was completed in 1827. It was the most expensive house in town, but Governor James B. Ray declined to move in. It was an unexpected complication, but it wasn't really complicated: While Ray governed the state for six years (1825–31), he did not govern the Ray household. His wife did. And she told him she would never live in a house on a hill with streets all around from which onlookers could peek through the windows. Moreover, she wanted no part of the city beholding the family laundry she'd have hanging on the clothesline in the backyard.

In fact, whether it was because of its fishbowl qualities or something else, no governor—and no governor's wife—would ever live in Alexander Ralston's centerpiece home. Instead, it was reduced to use at various times as office space for the state supreme court, the state library, the local medical

The Historic Memorial District of Downtown Indianapolis

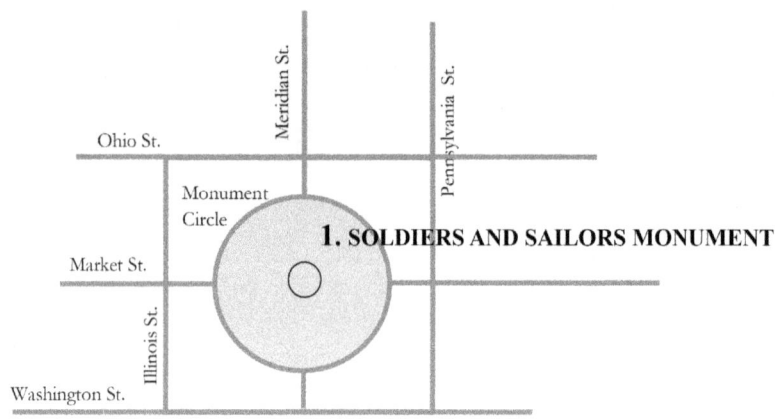

Map segment of Soldiers and Sailors Monument. *Map by Rudy Schouten.*

The governor's mansion on Monument Circle as sketched by Christian Schrader. *Bass Photo Co. Collection, Indiana Historical Society.*

Monument Circle street scene, Circle Park, circa 1880. *Bass Photo Co. Collection, Indiana Historical Society.*

society and a commercial bank. It was ultimately abandoned and left to serve as a haven for the homeless before it was torn down in 1857. When the mistake on the knoll was cleared away, Governor's Circle was reimagined as public space and renamed Circle Park.

INDIANAPOLIS AND THE CIVIL WAR

Meanwhile, the country was inching closer to the Civil War. While Indianapolis managed to stay out of the direct line of fire, its citizens played a significant role in the conduct of the bloody conflict. And the factors drawing the city into the fray would be among the first clues to its future in the monument business.

The population of Indianapolis grew quickly in the years leading up to the war—from eight thousand in 1850 to eighteen thousand in 1860. More and more of those living in the city worked in the city, many of them employed in manufacturing. But employment in the state was still based predominantly on agriculture, so state government began to take an interest in advancing new technology to promote improvements in farm productivity. To that end, it created the Indiana State Fair Board of Agriculture in 1851 and, in 1860, purchased a thirty-six-acre plot of ground bounded by Nineteenth Street, Twenty-Second Street, Talbott Street and Central Avenue, to develop a large, permanent site for a state fair.

But the Civil War broke out before the grounds were ready for the next fair date, and the land was seen as ideal property for a different use altogether—a training camp for recruits and then a prison camp for Confederate soldiers. By the summer of 1862, over four thousand prisoners were held there at the camp.

The city's location in the middle of the state and its emerging railways were also key factors in making Indianapolis so important to the Union. In addition to serving as the political and legislative center of the state's war effort, Indianapolis was well positioned as a gathering point for Hoosiers leaving for the war or coming home, and its rapidly expanding network of railroads helped the Union move troops and supplies quickly and efficiently to the battlefield.

Leadership was crucial, too. Republican Oliver P. Morton, a friend to President Abraham Lincoln and a powerful supporter of the Union cause, was Indiana's Civil War governor. The state had been settled largely by pioneers with southern roots, so there was some speculation that Indiana might side with the Confederacy, but it rallied firmly behind Morton and his leadership in support of the Union. Governor Morton was also known for his focus on making sure Hoosier soldiers had all the weapons, ammunition and supplies they needed to survive and to fight effectively. He went to great lengths to see to it that Hoosier soldiers were properly cared for in the field.

The Battle of Corydon (Morgan's Raid) was the only Civil War conflict waged on Indiana soil, but Hoosiers rallied to represent the Union in large numbers. Something in them, something about who they were and where they came from, needed to have a hand in the nation's destiny. Over 200,000 Hoosiers served in the war. More than 24,000 gave their lives to preserve the Union. Three out of every 4 Hoosiers eligible (by age) to serve did serve—the highest rate of participation for any state outside of Delaware. And, symbolically, the last Union soldier to perish in the war, Private John Williams, was from Portland, Indiana.

The state fair property (Camp Morton), the railroads in Indianapolis, the city's power base in central Indiana, Governor Morton and the surprising groundswell of Hoosier volunteer spirit were all part of the state's substantial contributions during the Civil War. People in Indianapolis, whether they were civic leaders or private citizens, noticed the sense of community and the sense of sacrifice, even before the war was over.

VISIONS OF A MONUMENT

In 1862, an article titled "Proposition" appeared in the *Indianapolis Daily Journal*. The author, named simply "Hoosier," proposed that "a monument be erected in Circle Park to all from Indiana who fell in defense of the Union." It was likely the first suggestion that a monument be built on the site of the old governor's mansion.

Five years later, Governor Morton tried to persuade the Indiana legislature to set aside funds to build a monument on the highest point in nearby Crown Hill Cemetery in honor of Hoosier soldiers protecting the Union. Another five years after that, William H. English, a prominent Indianapolis banker and member of the U.S. House of Representatives, and Major General Dan McCauley, a former mayor of Indianapolis, also pushed for resolutions to build a Civil War monument in Indianapolis. And, in 1875, a group of six Civil War veterans developed its own plan. The resolutions didn't all agree on a location for a monument, but they were consistent in the firm belief that it had to be built.

None of the initiatives succeeded, but they kept the conversation going until 1887, when the legislature issued a grant of $200,000 to build a memorial and appointed a monument commission. After considering a number of locations for the memorial, the act ordered the commissioners to build it "on the ground commonly known as Circle Park." In 1888, Bruno Schmitz, an architect from Berlin, won a competition among world-renowned architects submitting designs for the new monument, and he proposed an obelisk shaft made from Indiana limestone surrounded by pools, fountains and elaborate statuary. A vague notion swirling around in the city for years was finally linked to a plan, a concept and a location.

THE HISTORIC MEMORIAL DISTRICT OF DOWNTOWN INDIANAPOLIS

CONSTRUCTION TIMELINE IN A NUTSHELL

The central foundation of the monument was completed later in the same year by contractor Enos Hege of Indianapolis, and construction above ground began in earnest in 1889, when Schmitz arrived from Germany bearing his plaster model of the monument. Construction of the monument's terraces, approaches and superstructure proceeded quickly, and on August 22, 1889, the cornerstone was laid at the northeast corner of the monument. The Indiana Historical Society recounts the contents of a time capsule placed inside the cornerstone:

> *In it is a large copper box containing the complete reports of the adjutant general during the War for the Union which gives a list of all soldiers from Indiana who fought in the war. Also included are the rituals, badges, and rosters of the Grand Army of the Republic, the Woman's Relief Corps, the Sons of Veterans, and reports of many other organizations, copies of daily and weekly newspapers, and of the first and second constitutions of the State of Indiana, an impress of the Seal of State, the Acts of the General Assembly providing for the Monument, autographs of the Board of Commissioners for the monument, an American flag with thirty-eight stars, a photograph of the architect, Bruno Schmitz, and the program of the exercises at the cornerstone laying.*

Among those present for the laying of the cornerstone were Governor Alvin P. Hovey and President Benjamin Harrison. The inscription on the cornerstone reads:

August 22, 1889
ERECTED BY THE PEOPLE OF INDIANA
Act of General Assembly
March 3, 1887

The shaft of the Soldiers and Sailors Monument was completed in 1892, and the *Victory* sculpture (the crowning figure) was placed on top of the monument in the early fall of the following year. At that point, Circle Park was renamed Monument Place.

In 1894, cascade fountains, a modification to the original design of the base, were constructed on the east and west sides of the monument, and after a number of trial runs, an elevator was in place and ready for public use. In

A Walk along the Granite and the Limestone

Above: The Indiana Soldiers and Sailors Monument. Construction begins, circa 1889. *Bass Photo Co. Collection, Indiana Historical Society.*

Right: The Indiana Soldiers and Sailors Monument under construction and advertising, circa 1899. *Bass Photo Co. Collection, Indiana Historical Society.*

The Historic Memorial District of Downtown Indianapolis

Above, left: The Soldiers and Sailors Monument, looking to the north, shortly after construction, 1903. *Bass Photo Co. Collection, Indiana Historical Society.*

Above, right: The Soldiers and Sailors Monument, looking to the south in 1906. *Bass Photo Co. Collection, Indiana Historical Society.*

Left: The Soldiers and Sailors Monument, looking to the east in 1925. *Bass Photo Co. Collection, Indiana Historical Society.*

1895, the Army Astragal, the lowest and most elaborate of three decorative bronze bands surrounding the shaft of the monument, was placed into position. And in 1897, Austrian Rudolf Schwarz, Bruno Schmitz's principal sculptor on the monument project, arrived to carve the "War" and "Peace" groupings above the fountains.

A Walk along the Granite and the Limestone

Construction of the Soldiers and Sailors Monument was completed in 1901, and the structure was formally dedicated on May 15, 1902. Among those in attendance were General Lew Wallace; Indiana governor Winfield T. Durbin; Hoosier John W. Foster, who had been secretary of state under President Benjamin Harrison; and James Whitcomb Riley. The monument took twelve years to complete, and the cost of its design and construction was reported at just under $600,000.

A VIEW FROM THE STREET

The Indiana Soldiers and Sailors Monument is recognized internationally as one of the most outstanding achievements in architectural and sculptural art. It is the only Civil War monument in America dedicated to ordinary soldiers and sailors.

Base of the Soldiers and Sailors Monument, southeast quadrant of Monument Circle, in 1925. *Bass Photo Co. Collection, Indiana Historical Society.*

The Historic Memorial District of Downtown Indianapolis

Aerial view of the Soldiers and Sailors Monument and surroundings in 1938. *Bass Photo Co. Collection, Indiana Historical Society.*

The Soldiers and Sailors Monument looking to the northeast in 1950. *Bass Photo Co. Collection, Indiana Historical Society.*

A Walk along the Granite and the Limestone

The Soldiers and Sailors Monument looking to the southwest in 1965. *Bass Photo Co. Collection, Indiana Historical Society.*

Aerial view of the Soldiers and Sailors Monument and surroundings looking to the northwest in 1965. *Bass Photo Co. Collection, Indiana Historical Society.*

THE HISTORIC MEMORIAL DISTRICT OF DOWNTOWN INDIANAPOLIS

More recent postcard of the Soldiers and Sailors Monument. *Dexter Press, photo by John Penrod.*

A WALK ALONG THE GRANITE AND THE LIMESTONE

The monument's foundation is 30 feet deep, its base is 52 feet in diameter and the shaft rises 284 feet, 6 inches above the ground, just 15 feet shorter than the Statue of Liberty. It is distinctive for its elegant setting on the circle as well as its dramatic architecture, a blend of beautiful bronze sculptures set against a structure of gray oolitic limestone, a fine and durable stone quarried from Owen County, Indiana.

Our overview of the exterior of the Soldiers and Sailors Monument, at the intersection of Meridian and Market Streets, starts on the north side of the Circle.

North Elevation—Facing the North Side of the Monument

The Entrance

The stone steps leading to the entrance of the monument are seventy feet long. A large stone tablet above the bronze door commemorates Indiana's contributions to the War with Mexico (1846–48), the Indian and British War (1811–12), the War of the Revolution, the capture of Vincennes from the British (1779) and the Mexican Border Service. The inscription above the tablet bears a dedication: "To Indiana's Silent Victors."

Statue of William Henry Harrison, northeast quadrant of Monument Circle, as it appeared in 1905. *Bass Photo Co. Collection, Indiana Historical Society.*

The William Henry Harrison Statue

To the left, near the street and facing the northeast, stands a bronze statue of William Henry Harrison, the first governor of the Indiana territory. This statue is one of four such statues commemorating four epochs in Indiana's military history. Each of the four statues faces outward and is positioned between the converging points of the street intersections; Harrison's statue (northeast quadrant of the Circle) represents the Battle of Tippecanoe and the War of 1812. The cloak on Harrison's back was a late addition to the statue; sculptor John H. Mahoney of Indianapolis was not initially happy with his work, so his wife suggested the addition of the cloak to give Harrison's likeness greater distinction.

The Artillery Statue and the Sailor Statue

At the base of the monument, left of the entrance, stands a statue of an artilleryman, the first of four statues, one at each corner of the monument, representing branches of the military. To the right of the entrance stands a statue of a sailor. (The other two statues, representing an infantryman and a cavalry scout, anchor the south corners of the monument.) Each of the figures was carved out of a single block of limestone, and all were the work of German sculptor Rudolf Schwarz.

Bronze Candelabras (Lampposts)

Stone pedestals on opposite ends of the north steps hold large bronze candelabras, each forty feet high. The shafts are fluted in the shape of stalks of corn, and the fixtures feature a crest at the base bearing the words "E Pluribus Unum." A matching pair of candelabras anchors the steps on the south side of the monument.

Army Astragal

Three bronze astragals (ornate architectural projections) surround the shaft of the monument at different levels. The lowest one, seventy feet above the base, represents the army and illustrates the implements and the carnage of war. The Army Astragal, designed by Nicolaus Geiger of Germany, is sculpted with cannons, horses, flags and fallen soldiers. The north and south sides of the Army Astragal are similar, but on this side, a state seal, rather than a crest, appears between the eagle and the bison.

Navy Astragal

The second astragal, twelve feet above the first, is the Navy Astragal, representing the ships used in the war. The Navy Astragal, designed by George W. Brewster of Cleveland, features a sailor on the north side of the monument.

Date Astragal

The third and highest astragal on the monument, eighty feet above the Navy Astragal, is the Date Astragal. Also designed by George Brewster, this astragal has bronze panels bearing the years "1861" and "1865," the beginning and ending years of the Civil War. The Date Astragal on the north and west sides of the monument bears the year "1865," while "1861" appears on the south and east sides.

A Walk along the Granite and the Limestone

Above: North entrance to the monument as it appeared in 1907, showing inscriptions over the doorway and statues of an artilleryman (*left*) and a sailor (*right*). *Bass Photo Co. Collection, Indiana Historical Society.*

Right: Bronze lampposts on the north side of the monument as they appeared in 1930. *Bass Photo Co. Collection, Indiana Historical Society.*

The Historic Memorial District of Downtown Indianapolis

A Walk along the Granite and the Limestone

Opposite, top: The Army Astragal on the Soldiers and Sailors Monument from the northeast. *Photo by Rudy Schouten, 2019.*

Opposite, bottom: The Navy Astragal on the Soldiers and Sailors Monument from the northeast. *Photo by Rudy Schouten, 2019.*

Above: The Date Astragal on the Soldiers and Sailors Monument from the northeast. *Photo by Rudy Schouten, 2019.*

Capital

Eight stone eagles support the capital, the architectural top of the shaft and the enclosed observation deck, originally a turret nineteen feet high with a narrow surrounding "balcony."

Victory

Victory is the crowning figure gracing the top of the monument. It has also been variously known to native Hoosiers as "Lady Victory" or "Miss Indiana," names adopted for her early on, most likely by local writers and reporters. But when the monument was dedicated in 1902, T.C. Steele, who had been a member of the board responsible for selecting artists for the structure, expressed his clear preference for calling it *Victory*, which remains its more official name.

The *Victory* statue is the work of George W. Brewster, the man who created the Navy and Date Astragals. *Victory* stands on a bronze globe eight feet in diameter; it is thirty-eight feet tall and weighs 20,924 pounds. But from the north side of the monument, we see only its back; it faces the south.

East Elevation—Facing the East Side of the Monument

The Governor Oliver P. Morton Statue
To the left, near the street and facing the southeast, stands a statue of Oliver P. Morton, the second of the four bronze sculptures commemorating four epochs in Indiana's military history. Morton's statue, completed by Franklin Simmons, was part of Circle Park before the Soldiers and Sailors Monument was built and represents Indiana's Civil War history. It anchors the southeast quadrant of the Circle.

Fountain Candelabras (Lampposts)
On the east elevation, two large bronze candelabras at street level (set lower than the ones on the north and south steps) align with Market Street and feature bison and bears above water fountain basins. Two matching candelabras align with Market Street on the west side of the monument. In total, eight ornate bronze candelabras surround the monument.

Cascade Fountain
The cascade fountain on the east side of the monument is identical to the one on the west side. They were installed in 1894 to replace the original ones, which were deemed to be too small. Each fountain has a capacity of about seven thousand gallons of water per minute.

The "Dying Soldier" Statuary Group
The Dying Soldier statue appears just above the fountain on the monument. This grouping is the work of distinguished German sculptor Rudolf Schwarz and captures two comrades tending to a wounded soldier.

The "War" Statuary Group
Just above *The Dying Soldier* sculpture is the "War" statuary group. War is represented by "a battle scene showing cavalry and charging infantry and artillery. In the center the fierce goddess of war urges on the charge while Columbia in the background upholds the stars and stripes."

A Walk along the Granite and the Limestone

Left: Statue of Oliver P. Morton, southeast quadrant of Monument Circle, as it appeared in 1903. *Bass Photo Co. Collection, Indiana Historical Society.*

Below: *The Dying Soldier* statue, east elevation of the monument, as it appeared in 1939. *Bass Photo Co. Collection, Indiana Historical Society.*

The Historic Memorial District of Downtown Indianapolis

The "War" statuary group, east elevation of the monument, above the "Dying Soldier" grouping, as it appeared in 1903. *Bass Photo Co. Collection, Indiana Historical Society.*

The grouping represents our country's struggle for the Union. Bruno Schmitz was responsible for the original idea and the design for the elaborate "War" statuary group (as well as the "Peace" statuary group on the opposite side of the monument), but it was Rudolf Schwarz who ultimately carried out his designs. The "War" and the "Peace" groupings were each carved out of a single block of stone and took two years to complete.

Army Astragal
The Army Astragal on the east side of the monument continues the theme of the implements and the carnage of war.

Navy Astragal
The Navy Astragal on this side of the monument bears an image of the ship USS *Monitor*, a steam-powered ironclad warship built for the Union navy during the Civil War.

South Elevation—Facing the South Side of the Monument

The Entrance
As on the north side of the monument, the stone steps leading to the entrance are seventy feet long. A large stone tablet above the bronze door commemorates the Indiana Volunteers in the War for the Union (1861–65) and the War with Spain. As on the north entrance, an inscription above the tablet bears the dedication "To Indiana's Silent Victors."

The Governor James Whitcomb Statue
To the left, near the street and facing the southwest, stands a statue of Governor James Whitcomb, the third of the four bronze statues commemorating four epochs in Indiana's military history. Whitcomb's statue, designed by John H. Mahoney, represents the war with Mexico, as the war coincided with Whitcomb's administration.

The Infantry Statue and the Cavalry Statue
At the monument, left of the entrance stands a statue of an infantryman, the third of Rudolf Schwarz's four sculptures representing branches of the military. To the right of the entrance stands the fourth of the four, a cavalry scout.

As construction of the Soldiers and Sailors Monument proceeded, the commission established by the General Assembly to oversee its progress made a point of letting Rudolf Schwarz know they were very pleased with his sculptures but also noted that all the men in his artwork wore full beards. In reality, during the time of the Civil War, most young soldiers would have been clean-shaven or wore only closely cropped beards. The sculptures of the soldiers were deemed "too German," so Schwarz patiently went back to work with his chisel to shave their faces.

THE HISTORIC MEMORIAL DISTRICT OF DOWNTOWN INDIANAPOLIS

Right: Statue of Governor James Whitcomb, southwest quadrant of Monument Circle, as it appeared in 1915. *Bass Photo Co. Collection, Indiana Historical Society.*

Below: South entrance to the monument as it appeared in 1914, showing inscriptions over the doorway and statues of the infantryman (*left*) and the cavalry scout (*right*). *Bass Photo Co. Collection, Indiana Historical Society.*

A Walk along the Granite and the Limestone

Bronze Candelabras
Large bronze candelabras set on stone pedestals on opposite ends of the south steps mirror the two on the north side of the monument to form a square of four massive candelabras, one for each corner of the base.

Army Astragal
The Army Astragal on the south side of the monument is identical to the one on the north side, with one exception: A crest with stars and stripes, not a state seal, appears between the eagle and the bison.

Navy Astragal
The Navy Astragal on this side of the monument features boat hulls modeled after Admiral David Farragut's Union flagship, the *Hartford*.

Victory
Victory faces the south, it is widely believed, to welcome Hoosier soldiers

The crowning figure *Victory* and the capital atop the Soldiers and Sailors Monument from the northeast. *Photo by Rudy Schouten, 2019.*

home from the war—or Southerners back into the Union. But an alternate theory suggests that the statue has its hand up to implore Confederates never to leave the Union again. Travel literature provided by the State of Indiana offers a poetic description of her purpose:

> *In Lady Victory's right hand is a sword, the top of which rests upon a globe: this symbolizes the army to which victory was due. Her left hand holds a torch, gleaming with gold, which represents the light of civilization. The young eagle on her brow is emblematic of freedom.*

West Elevation—Facing the West Side of the Monument

George Rogers Clark Statue

To the left, near the street and facing the northwest, stands a statue of George Rogers Clark, the last of the four bronze statues commemorating four epochs in Indiana's military history. Clark, who represents the Revolution, is shown as the fearless commander of the small band of soldiers at the capture of Fort Sackville. The Clark statue, designed by John H. Mahoney, is on the northwest quadrant of the Circle.

Cascade Fountain

The cascade fountain on the west side of the monument, like the one on the east, was installed in 1894 and has a capacity of seven thousand gallons per minute.

The "Return Home" Statuary Group

The *Return Home* statue appears just above the fountain on the monument. Also sculpted by Rudolf Schwarz, this statuary grouping captures the reunion of a soldier and his family. The plow represents the tools of peaceful labor.

The "Peace" Statuary Group

Just above the *Return Home* sculpture is the "Peace" sculptural group. Like the *War* sculpture on the opposite side of the monument, it was designed by Bruno Schmitz and sculpted by Rudolf Schwarz. The grouping represents the peace and prosperity that followed the struggle for the Union. A pamphlet by the Indiana War Memorials Commission describes additional significance of the statuary:

Statue of George Rogers Clark, northwest quadrant of Monument Circle, as it appeared in 1929. *Bass Photo Co. Collection, Indiana Historical Society.*

The Historic Memorial District of Downtown Indianapolis

Above: The "Peace" and the "Return Home" statuary groupings, west elevation of the monument, as they appeared in 1903. *Bass Photo Co. Collection, Indiana Historical Society.*

Left: Closer view of the "Peace" and "Return Home" statuary groupings, west elevation of the monument, with cascade fountain in use; photo is undated. *Bass Photo Co. Collection, Indiana Historical Society.*

A Walk along the Granite and the Limestone

Base of the monument's west elevation (looking east) showing the "Peace" and "Return Home" statuary groupings, six bronze lampposts and the Army and Navy Astragals as they appeared in 1930. *Bass Photo Co. Collection, Indiana Historical Society.*

> *Peace represents the homecoming of the victorious troops, the happy reunion of families, and the peaceful emblems of labor. In the center Liberty upholds the flag while at her feet the freed slave lifts up his broken chains. The angel of Peace, hovering over the scene holds aloft the wreath of Victory and the olive branch of peace.*

Army Astragal
The Army Astragal on the west side of the monument continues the theme of the implements and the carnage of war.

Navy Astragal
The Navy Astragal on the west side of the monument bears an image of the ship CSS *Virginia*, converted from the hull of the frigate USS *Merrimac*, an ironclad ship in the Confederate navy during the Civil War. The first

The Historic Memorial District of Downtown Indianapolis

The Soldiers and Sailors Monument from the northeast. *Photo by Rudy Schouten, 2019.*

American warship of its kind, it met its match, the USS *Monitor*, at the Battle of Hampton Roads in 1862.

WEARING WELL

The monument has taken on the abuse of age and the elements, but it looks very much today as it did on completion in 1902. A few changes have been made to the structure over the years, however. A museum was opened in the basement in 1918. Floodlighting was added to the candelabra fixtures in 1928 to highlight the monument at night. The observation level of the monument, originally an outdoor platform, was enclosed for the first time in 1936, which necessitated the removal of the cornice and the turret at the base of the *Victory* statue. Flower gardens replaced grass-covered spaces in 1956. The monument was decorated for the holiday season for the first time in 1962. And the Colonel Eli Lilly Civil War Museum, which opened below the main shaft of the monument in 1999, has more recently been relocated to the Indiana War Memorial.

But most of the work on the Soldiers and Sailors Monument has been focused on preserving it for future generations. In the 1940s and 1950s, workmen routinely climbed into *Victory* to repair and maintain the crowning statue. A large-scale effort to renovate the monument was launched in the late 1980s, including the installation of climate control, a new elevator and a new glass-and-aluminum enclosure on the observation deck. Work also included essential repairs and a major cleaning of the interior and exterior of the monument. And in 2011, for the first time since its placement on top of the monument in 1893, *Victory* was removed and lowered from the monument for a complete restoration and repair. It was back in place by November, just in time for the annual Circle of Lights celebration and the 2012 Super Bowl, held for the first time in Indianapolis.

STOP 2
UNIVERSITY PARK

IN SEARCH OF A PURPOSE

Alexander Ralston's vision for the site of today's University Park missed the mark, in the long run, by as much as his plans for the Governor's Circle. His original city plat in 1821 had Square 25, just north of the U.S. Post Office and Courthouse building, divided into twelve lots with alleys running midway through the block in both directions. But like the rest of the original Mile Square, the lots didn't initially sell like hotcakes. So, in 1827, the Indiana General Assembly, in an effort to make better use of the property, vacated the alleys and set the land aside for use as a state university, and the four-acre square was renamed University Square.

The first school building on the property, however, wouldn't be completed for another seven years. In 1834, the new Marion County Seminary, a school for young men offering a curriculum that "approached collegiate quality," opened for business in the southwest corner of the park. The two-story brick structure fronting New York Street also hosted church groups that held Sunday services on the first floor.

The legislature tried for many years to lease the remaining land in University Square to other educational institutions, without much success, and the Marion County Seminary, which had struggled from the outset, closed its doors in 1844. The building remained empty for another nine years before reopening as the city's first public high school, which then survived on the site for only five years.

A Walk along the Granite and the Limestone

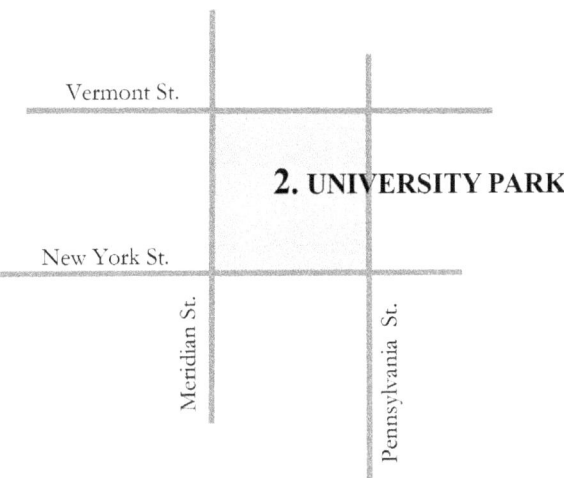

Map segment of University Park. *Map by Rudy Schouten.*

The Marion County Seminary building in University Square, circa 1860. *Bass Photo Co. Collection, Indiana Historical Society.*

The seminary remained as the only structure on the block until 1860, when entrepreneur J.B. Perrine enclosed a portion of the square with a high fence and built a large "shed." The "Coliseum," as he called it, would be "a rendezvous for political assemblies, shows, circuses, and the like." The facility was billed as "big enough to hold 20,000 people" at a time when it was reported the city had fewer than that number capable of paying an admission fee. The Coliseum opened with a big show on July 4 that year, but by the time September rolled around, both the shed and the seminary building had been razed.

The timing was right for University Square to stumble into a new use. The land, now free of encumbrances, was a good place for Indiana volunteers to train for the Civil War and demonstrate the state's loyalty to the Union. In late 1860, it became the drill grounds for the Nineteenth Regular U.S. Infantry. In 1863, when John Morgan and his Confederate cavalry raided southern Indiana to stir up suspected Confederate sympathies, University Square was used as a parade ground for the Indiana Home Guard.

After the war, residents in the vicinity raised funds to develop Square 25 as a park suitable for enhancing the setting of their elaborate homes. They spent $3,000 to grade the land, plant grass and trees and surround the park with a high iron picket fence to keep the cows and the vandals out. Meanwhile, the residents of Bloomington, Indiana, were staking a claim to the same ground, because "land set aside for use as a state university" should, after all, belong to the state university already firmly in place in Bloomington. A Special Study Commission appointed by the legislature in 1867 to settle the dispute decided that the land should be reserved "until such time as it was needed for a state university" and then eventually authorized the city, more officially, to make a park of University Square "until such time as a better use could be found for it."

No better use was ever found. Nearly ten years later, in 1876, plans for a city park became a reality when the picket fence was removed and the first sidewalks were installed. The layout of those walkways would be altered aesthetically from time to time for a few years, but the concept—walking paths connecting to the streets from a center point—would not.

The park's first statue, the likeness of Schuyler Colfax, was completed and dedicated in 1887, and in 1895, the state legislature handed jurisdiction of the park over to the Indianapolis Board of Park Commissioners, which has maintained it ever since as University Park.

The new University Park, established seven years *before* the dedication of the Soldiers and Sailors Monument just two blocks to the south, would be

University Park, with the Soldiers and Sailors Monument in the distance, as it appeared in 1922. *Bass Photo Co. Collection, Indiana Historical Society*.

the first piece and the southern anchor for the future Indiana War Memorial Plaza. But it wasn't until after a redesign of the park by George Kessler in 1914 that it began to assume its present appearance, and the last memorial to be built on the property, the Lincoln statue, wasn't completed and dedicated until 1935. Starting with the pouring of the original sidewalks, construction of University Park was a sixty-year project.

A VIEW FROM THE STREET

Our walk through University Park starts on New York Street, the southern edge of the park, midway between Meridian and Pennsylvania Streets.

President Benjamin Harrison Statue
Facing New York Street to the south stands a sculpture of Benjamin Harrison, our nation's twenty-third president (1889–93) and the only

The Historic Memorial District of Downtown Indianapolis

Right: Benjamin Harrison Monument, on the southern edge of University Park, as it appeared in 1908. *Bass Photo Co. Collection, Indiana Historical Society.*

Opposite: The Benjamin Harrison statue at the southern edge of University Park. *Photo by Rudy Schouten, 2018.*

American president from Indiana. Harrison was the grandson of William Henry Harrison, the ninth president.

Designed by architect Henry Bacon and sculpted by Charles Niehaus of New York, the statue portrays Harrison in a full-length coat holding eyeglasses in one hand and rolled-up papers in the other. The sculpture is set on a stone pedestal bearing an image of an eagle and a listing of Harrison's achievements. At the base, a quote from the noted orator is carved into the stone: "Great lives do not go out, they go on." An elevated stone bench wraps around the back of the monument. The memorial was dedicated in 1908.

A Fading Relic

To the left of the Harrison statue, embedded in the ground in the southwest corner of the block, a worn piece of limestone marks the site of the old Marion County Seminary building. The stone once bore a plaque, a gift from a few proud graduates of the school, paying tribute to the building's short history as a school. It read: "Location of Marion County Seminary 1833–1853—Placed here July 17, 1878 by the living teachers and scholars in memory of their dead comrades."

President Abraham Lincoln Statue
To the right, in the southeast corner of the park, facing the intersection of New York and Pennsylvania Streets, is a bronze sculpture of a seated Abraham Lincoln. The Civil War president is portrayed with a hand outstretched, as if to calm a nation at war. Indiana Civil War veteran Henry

Abraham Lincoln statue, southeast corner of University Park, as it appeared (in the snow) in 1936. *Bass Photo Co. Collection, Indiana Historical Society.*

Clay Long, who died in 1901, had stipulated in his will that $10,000 of his estate be used to build a statue of Lincoln in University Park. But city officials, believing the statue would be inappropriate for the park, tried to have the money reallocated for other uses. Thirty years later, the courts ruled that the fund, which had grown to about $17,000, would be used as originally specified, and the work was begun.

The statue, designed by Henry Hering, also of New York, was completed in 1934 and dedicated on April 6, 1935. It stands in the middle of a widened section of one of the diagonal sidewalks forming the pattern in George Kessler's park design. The statue's handsome granite base is relatively unadorned. The front, near the top, bears only the name "Abraham Lincoln" in gold, while the back credits "Citizen Henry Long" for his gift to the city. Behind and under the chair sits Lincoln's hat and gloves.

The question of why Lincoln's statue was, after all, appropriate for University Square in Indianapolis, Indiana, was addressed by Dr. Louis A.

The Abraham Lincoln statue at the southeast corner of University Park. *Photo Courtesy Rudy Schouten, 2018.*

Warren, director of the Lincoln National Life Foundation and principal speaker at the dedication:

> *Many people do not know that Abraham Lincoln spent nearly one fourth of his life in Indiana—and the most impressionable years at that....Lincoln exemplifies Indiana. He was born in the year Indiana became a territory; he came to Indiana in 1816, when it achieved statehood....He was here from his seventh year to his twenty-first, and when he left he was not an ignorant boy, but a well-read young man able to cope with the best of Illinois politicians.*

Schuyler Colfax Statue

A short walk north on Pennsylvania leads to the east–west spoke in University Park's sidewalk grid, halfway between New York and Vermont Streets. To the left, looking into the east-central portion of the park, stands the towering statue of Schuyler Colfax, U.S. representative for Indiana's Ninth Congressional District from 1855 to 1869 and U.S. vice president under Ulysses S. Grant from 1869 to 1873. The Indiana native, known for his strong opposition to slavery, was also a founder of the Republican Party and U.S. Speaker of the House from 1863 to 1869.

As with the Harrison statue, Colfax is depicted wearing a full-length coat over a suit and holding rolled-up papers in his left hand. The bronze statue, resting on a tall, multi-tiered pedestal of granite, is identified at its base simply as "COLFAX." Just below the top tier of columns, "I.O.O.F." refers to the Independent Order of Odd Fellows, a humanitarian organization with roots in seventeenth-century England. Colfax was a distinguished member of the group and wrote its "Rebekah Creed" in 1851, making the I.O.O.F. the first national fraternal organization to include both men and women. The plaque below the acronym depicts the biblical Isaac and Rebekah at the well, representing kindness and hospitality to a stranger.

The Colfax statue, designed in Chicago by Illinois sculptor Lorado Taft, was the first piece of statuary placed in University Park, but it has a somewhat nomadic history. When it was dedicated in 1887, it stood in a sidewalk in the southwest corner of the park, near the site of the old Marion County Seminary. In 1919, it was moved to the north side of the park to comply with George Kessler's 1914 redesign of the square, which included a recommendation that the Colfax statue be lined up as a bookend to the Benjamin Harrison statue on the opposite side. But in 1930, after completion of the Indiana World War Memorial, it was moved to its present location on the east-central portion of the park, out of the open sightlines desired for the center of the mall and the War Memorial Building.

A Walk along the Granite and the Limestone

Above: The Schuyler Colfax statue, University Park, as it appeared in 1909. *Bass Photo Co. Collection, Indiana Historical Society.*

Opposite, inset: Postcard (mailed in 1906) of the Schuyler Colfax Monument in University Park. *A.C. Bosselman & Co., New York.*

The Historic Memorial District of Downtown Indianapolis

Depew Memorial Fountain

Behind the Colfax statue, in the middle of Square 25, is the Depew Fountain, the elaborate centerpiece of University Park. Depew Memorial Fountain, the successor to a more modest fountain in the square, was a gift to the city of Indianapolis from Emma Ely Depew. When she died in 1913, she had bequeathed $50,000 of her estate to the city for the construction of a memorial to her husband, well-known Indianapolis physician Dr. Richard J. Depew, who had died in 1887.

Construction of the memorial began in 1913 and is the work of three notables in early twentieth-century public art. Henry Bacon, a landscape architect, designed the memorial's setting, and Karl Bitter, an Austrian-born American sculptor, designed and created the fountain. Bitter was killed in a traffic accident in New York City in 1915, well before the work was finished, so Alexander Stirling Calder, a sculptor from Philadelphia, continued with the work on the memorial, following Bitter's original designs. The fountain was completed in 1919.

The monument features a five-tier pink Stony Creek granite base with three basins. The bronze sculptures include fish, a circle of eight dancing

Above: Fountain in University Square, pre-dating Depew Fountain in University Park. *Bass Photo Co. Collection, Indiana Historical Society.*

Opposite, top: Depew Fountain in University Park as it appeared in 1921. *Bass Photo Co. Collection, Indiana Historical Society.*

Opposite, bottom: Depew Fountain in University Park, with Chamber of Commerce Building in the background, as it appeared in 1932. *Bass Photo Co. Collection, Indiana Historical Society.*

A Walk along the Granite and the Limestone

children and a crowning figure of a woman smiling and dancing as she plays the cymbals. The design was a reflection of Emma Ely's specific wishes for the memorial: As a reaction to the elitism she experienced in life, and her aversion to it, she asked that the park be created as a welcoming place for the common Hoosier. A plaque on top of the wall surrounding the main basin on the south side of the memorial reads:

> *Depew Memorial Fountain—A Gift to Indianapolis from Emma Ely Depew in memory of her husband Richard Johnson Depew M.D. whose long and honorable life was spent in untiring service to his fellow men.*

To the east and west of the fountain are sculptures of Pan and Syrinx, framing a theme to the memorial based in Greek mythology. The bookends to the Depew memorial have a mysterious past. Early in the history of University Park, a traveling salesman who lived in the neighborhood left $1,500 to the city for the construction of a drinking fountain. The parks department matched the $1,500 to tally enough for two of them—one for

Depew Memorial Fountain in 2018. *Photo by Rudy Schouten.*

A Walk along the Granite and the Limestone

Statues of Pan (*left*) and Syrinx (*right*) at Depew Memorial Fountain in 2018. *Photos by Rudy Schouten.*

University Park looking south, with the Federal Building in the background, as it appeared in 1944. *Bass Photo Co. Collection, Indiana Historical Society.*

the east side and one for the west side of Depew Memorial Fountain. Myra Richards, a local sculptress, was commissioned to create the fountains as well as a small statue to "repose" atop each one.

Above the fountain to the west she created the figure of Pan, the Greek god of shepherds and flocks, depicted as a satyr (a half-human, half-beast deity of the woods and mountains). Satyrs typically held a reed pipe, a shepherd's crook and a branch of pine and were known to spend their time drinking, dancing and chasing nymphs. Richards had her sculpture facing east, piping his tune to the dancing children and the woman atop the Depew fountain. Above the drinking fountain on the east side of the memorial, she sculpted Syrinx, the graceful wood nymph watching the children dance and listening for her companion Pan's music coming from the opposite side.

Myra Richards's statuettes were completed in 1923, but the Pan and Syrinx sculptures seen in University Park today are not the originals; Syrinx disappeared in 1959 and Pan in 1970, during a period in which the park had fallen into some disrepair. Replacements in the form of new designs,

Depew Fountain and University Park looking north. *Photo by Rudy Schouten, 2018.*

bronze figures on limestone pedestals, were sculpted by Adolph Wolter in 1973. And while Wolter's version of Syrinx survives to this day, the popular Pan figure was stolen again—and again. The fourth sculpture of Pan, the current version, was created by American sculptor Roger White in 2005.

THE LAND NO LONGER IN LIMBO

Square 25 took a while to find its purpose, but once those first presumptive pieces were in place—the things that looked suspiciously like something you'd see in a park—the land turned inexorably into what it is today. It has gone through a number of transformations, including landscaping makeovers and a major rejuvenation in the 1970s, when new lighting was added to the park. But it continues to look much like the vision George Kessler had for it when he formed the city's parks and boulevards.

STOP 3
INDIANA WAR MEMORIAL

A CHANGING LANDSCAPE

Like University Park, the block north of it in Alexander Ralston's plat of Indianapolis, Square 16, began as a grid of twelve separate lots and ended up serving a more singular purpose. It would become home to the Indiana World War Memorial. And while, ultimately, neither of the two squares of the city grid followed neatly into Ralston's plans, there were significant differences in how they were transformed into what they would become. Unlike the beginnings of University Park, the Indiana World War Memorial block never resembled a relatively blank slate to work from; it boasted a generation of fine homes for the elite, then a mix of public and commercial buildings occupying nearly every one of its original lots. The memorial had a dense grid of structures in its path.

FORERUNNERS ON THE BLOCK

The 1924 R.L. Polk City Directory hints at the long-gone bustle inside the block bounded by Vermont, Meridian, Michigan and Pennsylvania Streets—hotels, apartment buildings, insurance companies, tailors, building suppliers, social clubs, ad agencies, legal offices and much more. Original plans called for removing all fourteen buildings on the square.

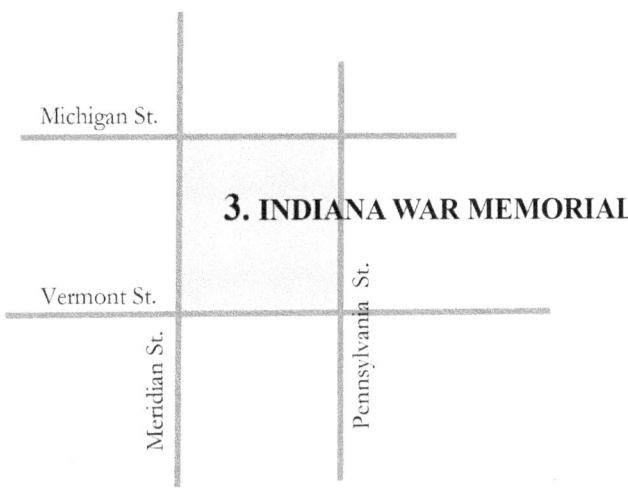

Map segment of Indiana War Memorial. *Map by Rudy Schouten.*

The most prominent ones stood on the north and south ends of the block. On the southern boundary, churches bookended the Vermont Street block. The First Baptist Church (2–10 East Vermont) stood at the northeast corner of Vermont and Meridian Streets. The landmark stone structure, built in 1904, featured a red-tile roof, large and distinctive church windows fronting both Vermont and Meridian Streets and, a novelty at the time, electric lighting in its steeple. And just east of the First Baptist Church stood the five-story Bobbs-Merrill Publishing Company Building (18 East Vermont). Bobbs-Merrill published codified state laws, schoolbooks and a long string of novels that were U.S. top-ten sellers.

Nestled in between the Bobbs-Merrill Building and North Scioto, the alley running midway between Meridian and Pennsylvania Streets, stood a large brick house (22 East Vermont) overlooking University Park. It was typical of the first generation of structures on the block; impressive homes standing among the city's generous inventory of churches. The home, built in the 1880s and occupied by members of the Claypool family, leaders in the city's early hotel industry, had survived the commercial transformation of the block, at least to this point. East of the alley, at 30 East Vermont, stood another residence of the same era, at this point the home of Elks Club Lodge No. 13.

The Historic Memorial District of Downtown Indianapolis

Above: The First Baptist Church as it appeared in 1920, before construction of the Indiana World War Memorial. A portion of the Bobbs-Merrill Building appears to the right of the church. *Bass Photo Co. Collection, Indiana Historical Society.*

Right: Democratic Club as it appeared in 1911. *Bass Photo Co. Collection, Indiana Historical Society.*

Elks Club Lodge No. 13 on Vermont Street, prior to construction of the Indiana World War Memorial. *Bass Photo Co. Collection, Indiana Historical Society.*

The Historic Memorial District of Downtown Indianapolis

Left: The Second Presbyterian Church, as it appeared in 1903. *Bass Photo Co. Collection, Indiana Historical Society*.

Below; The Cambridge Apartment House, 21 East Michigan Street, as it appeared in 1907. *Bass Photo Co. Collection, Indiana Historical Society*.

Closing out the block on the opposite end of Vermont was the Second Presbyterian Church (36–38 East Vermont) at the northwest corner of Vermont and Pennsylvania Streets. The Second Presbyterian Church was once referred to as the "Henry Ward Beecher Church," because the celebrated preacher had been the congregation's first pastor in 1839. The church's first services were held in the old Marion County Seminary in University Square, but the first church building they could call their own stood in the northwest quadrant of Monument Circle. The version of the Second Presbyterian Church sharing the block with the War Memorial Plaza was built in the late 1860s.

Notable buildings on the north end of Square 16 included the six-story Haugh Hotel at 11 East Michigan Street, just west of the alley. Delano Flats and the Cambridge Apartment House, which sat on the southwest corner of Michigan and Pennsylvania Streets, anchored Michigan Street east of the alley.

THE EVOLUTION OF AN IDEA

All those old buildings and the people who lived and worked there were just going about their business when the rumblings began—when a big idea began to unfold. Although, really, it was an idea with roots dating back half a century. Indiana's outsized role in the Civil War and the city's early, active interest in honoring the military and those who served helped Indianapolis earn a certain reputation nationally. Local and federal interests aligned, and a confluence of circumstances was beginning to steer the city into a unique identity.

In 1903, Congress authorized the establishment of Fort Benjamin Harrison north of Indianapolis—headquarters, barracks, officers' quarters, a hospital, stables and other support buildings for the army's Tenth Infantry Regiment. The construction, which was completed in 1910, was both a demonstration and a reflection of the state's ongoing commitment to service to the nation.

During roughly the same time frame (1902–5), in the heart of Indianapolis, work was underway on the original configuration of the grand United States Court House and Post Office at Meridian and Ohio Streets, now the Birch Bayh Federal Building and United States Court House (District Court for the Southern District of Indiana). The limestone Beaux-Arts structure

The Historic Memorial District of Downtown Indianapolis

and its classic features would be an ideal architectural complement to the beautiful James Whitcomb Riley Library building to the north (now the central branch of the Indianapolis Public Library), which would open in 1917. And the half mile of real estate between the two would frame the canvas for the big idea, rounding more completely into view in the pre-armistice days of World War I.

Late in 1918, American servicemen overseas began talking about forming civilian groups to help them stay connected after the war and to help them find ways to serve their country in civilian life. A few months later, in February 1919, Theodore Roosevelt Jr. and a few officers met in Paris to discuss the postwar needs of American servicemen, which led to a March caucus in Paris of one thousand officers and enlisted men. They had gathered to formulate plans for a great society of American world war veterans. It was the birth of the American Legion.

Back home, some fifty years after Governor Oliver Morton suggested the state build a monument to those who died to protect the union, a new generation of civic-minded Hoosiers suggested the idea of building a memorial to those from Indiana who had served in the Great War. The idea was to "have a park or plaza in the heart of the state's capital, providing for future generations a breathing space with grass, trees, shrubbery and beautiful buildings as a relief from the rush and bustle of the busy thoroughfares."

After a brief planning session in St. Louis, the newly minted American Legion held its first national convention in November 1919 in Minneapolis, where it approved a constitution and set out to decide on a permanent home. Roosevelt brought the Legion, at least temporarily, to his native New York, but Legion members from throughout the country were not all especially enamored of the idea of traveling to the East Coast on a regular basis to conduct business. Despite strong, competitive bidding from four other cities (Minneapolis, Kansas City, Detroit and Washington, D.C.), an aggressive campaign by the delegation from the state of Indiana convinced the membership to locate the American Legion's national headquarters in Indianapolis.

Some old-fashioned arm-twisting, a little bit of politics, a strong tradition of support for the military and a demonstrated culture of civic duty were all influential considerations in the decision to bring the Legion to Indianapolis. But the biggest factors falling in the city's favor were its location in the heart of the country and the impressive network of railways flowing in and out of its Union Station. Indianapolis was already the "Crossroads of America," and it had nothing to do with interstate highways.

And if the delegation had an ace in the hole to help put it over the top in the bidding, it was the city's growing commitment to building an impressive war memorial that could stand impressively next to the Legion's new headquarters.

Indiana didn't waste any time taking the honor and the opportunity seriously. In 1920, a Citizens Planning Committee set aside two blocks, Square 16 and the block to the north (Square 5), for use in constructing a memorial. A special session of the Indiana General Assembly then created the Indiana World War Memorial, a larger tract "to honor those who served in WWI as well as to provide a suitable building for the National Headquarters of the American Legion." The State of Indiana, Marion County and the City of Indianapolis all pitched in to set aside space for the project: the five blocks between the library and the U.S. Courthouse; more specifically, the area bounded by Meridian, St. Clair, Pennsylvania and New York Streets.

The state would pay for memorial construction by placing a tax of "six tenths of a cent on each one hundred dollars valuation of property for a period of twelve years." The city would provide funding for the purchase of the land and ongoing maintenance of the properties. Business concerns and private citizens would share in the cost, too— not just in the form of their tax dollars but by incurring the inconvenience and the expense of the disruptions and dislocations resulting from the construction and by getting behind the project. It would be a community effort, and community leaders were well aware of the benefits it would bring to the state: new business, new economic opportunity, enhanced community spirit and a stronger sense of identity for Hoosiers. What's more, according to Walter Myers, the 1918 Democratic candidate for mayor, "the presence of the American Legion headquarters in Indianapolis makes the city the 'Capital of Patriotism.'" Bringing all of that to fruition would be a painful and painstaking process, but it was not undertaken without sound, thoughtful planning. Indiana was fortunate enough to have the right people in place at exactly the right time. And while city and state leaders would not have known it by its present name, they may well have been the authors of one of the first economic development initiatives in the city's history.

CLEARING THE WAY

Square 16, the site of the proposed Indiana World War Memorial, would be the focal point of the grand plan. But the ground on which the memorial was to stand was otherwise occupied. So, in 1922, Marion County bought every piece of property on the block, except for the two churches bookending the Vermont Street side of the square. The rest would have a date with either a wrecking ball or a company clever and brazen enough to move it.

A news article in early 1926 reported that the Bobbs-Merrill Building, the relatively new structure next door to the First Baptist Church, would be torn down. But it was saved at the last minute by a local realtor who bought the building from the War Memorial Commission and had it moved to 122 East Michigan Street, the north side of the street, where it found new life in 1928 as the Indiana University Extension Center and offices for center director Professor R.E. Cavanaugh and his staff. The building stood until 1971, when it was demolished to make room for the Minton-Capehart Federal Building.

The stately old house east of the Bobbs-Merrill Building had become headquarters of the Indiana Democratic Club in 1911, and its members added a parlor to the front of the house a year later. But like the house across the alley hosting the Elks Club and the few remaining residential structures on the block, the Indiana Democratic Club was razed and out of the way by 1926.

But the gradual decline in the number of beautiful homes in the area and the subsequent demolition of those that remained didn't mean there was no need for housing. Actually, the opposite was true. Indianapolis experienced a housing boom in the 1920s, but people were moving into apartments, not houses, so apartment buildings, particularly those along the north end of Square 16, were a hot commodity and worth the trouble of saving if humanly possible.

In one of the more ambitious relocations, the six-story Haugh Hotel, which had been built only ten years earlier, was moved east one block to 127 East Michigan Street, where it became the Michigan Apartments. The building was too long, front to back, to travel down the street in its north–south orientation, so it was rotated one-quarter turn to face east for the trip across Pennsylvania Street and then rotated back to face north as it was backed into its new location. "The Mich" survives in Indy's landscape and is now best known for the sixty-foot mural of Reggie Miller, the former Indiana Pacer star, painted on the exterior brick on the east side of the building.

Later in the same year, November 1926, the Cambridge Apartment House, resting comfortably on the southwest corner of Pennsylvania and Michigan Streets, found itself on the move, too. The Cambridge, at just three stories tall, was a slightly more manageable relocation project than the Haugh Hotel had been, but it had to travel a little farther. A report in the

A Walk along the Granite and the Limestone

Left: The Haugh Hotel; preparations underway for moving the building to its new location. *Bass Photo Co. Collection, Indiana Historical Society.*

Right: The old Haugh Hotel, renamed the Hotel Michigan, in its new location at 127 East Michigan Street in 1960. *Bass Photo Co. Collection, Indiana Historical Society.*

Indianapolis News began with the Cambridge already parked in the middle of Michigan Street: "Trolley wires will be severed in Pennsylvania Street while the building is moved in the still hours of the morning. Movers expect to have the building on the other side of the street and street car service restored by 5 a.m. At Michigan and Delaware streets the Cambridge will make a left turn and travel to the northwest corner of North and Delaware streets, its future site."

In those days, crowds of curious onlookers marveled at the spectacle of large buildings "trundled" to new locations like a "Checkerboard of Progress." But it was the kind of insanity that made some sense. According to the *News*, "those big buildings were placed on rollers and moved for city blocks without even cracking the plaster or loosening a brick."

All told, sixteen buildings were removed from Square 16 in preparation for the construction of the Indiana World War Memorial. The south half of the two blocks set aside for the project lost a few pieces of its history and a trove of beautiful buildings, all in the space of a couple of years. The sacrifice was a painful process to comprehend at the time, and maybe even more so in hindsight, but it would yield the crown jewel of the plaza.

THE HISTORIC MEMORIAL DISTRICT OF DOWNTOWN INDIANAPOLIS

A RISING MEMORIAL

Preliminary work on the plaza began in 1921, when the newly appointed War Memorial Board launched a nationwide competition for an architect and a design concept that would "commemorate valor and the sacrifices of soldiers, sailors, and marines while also providing meeting, office and archival space." From the twenty-six firms submitting proposals, the board selected Frank B. Walker and Harry E. Weeks, architects from Cleveland, Ohio, to carry out the project. Additional planning and the work of negotiating settlements with property owners took four years, but preparations for

Above: Foundation work underway for the Indiana World War Memorial (Building "A"), July 6, 1926. The First Baptist Church stands in the background, in the upper left. *Photo courtesy of the Indiana War Memorials Commission.*

Opposite, top: The new Indiana World War Memorial Building begins to rise above the ground, May 31, 1927. The U.S. Post Office and Courthouse appears in the upper left, on the opposite side of University Park. *Photo courtesy of the Indiana War Memorials Commission.*

Opposite, bottom: The Indiana World War Memorial begins to take shape, November 14, 1927. *Photo courtesy of the Indiana War Memorials Commission.*

A Walk along the Granite and the Limestone

building the monument could finally begin in 1925, and construction began early the following year.

Construction moved quickly, at least initially. The cornerstone was laid on July 4, 1927, by four-star General John J. Pershing, and the iconic bronze sculpture on the south side of the monument, the *Pro Patria* statue, was set in place in 1929. But delays in state funding in the late 1920s and early 1930s, a consequence of politics and the economy, slowed completion of the exterior of the building. The Shrine Room, the centerpiece of the interior, was dedicated on November 11, 1933, but the monument itself would wait another four years to be so honored. After ceremonies were postponed twice (Armistice Day 1936 and in April 1937) to permit completion of various parts of the structure, the dedication was finally set for July 4, 1937, when the memorial was still not entirely complete.

In fact, Indiana's memorial to those who served in the Great War would not be complete, as envisioned by the architects, for another thirty years.

The Indiana World War Memorial under construction in 1928, looking to the north, with University Park in the foreground. *Bass Photo Co. Collection, Indiana Historical Society.*

A Walk along the Granite and the Limestone

Left: Construction of the Indiana World War Memorial is nearly complete, May 21, 1928. *Photo courtesy of the Indiana War Memorials Commission.*

Below: Construction continues on the south stairs of the Indiana World War Memorial, September 10, 1928. *Photo courtesy of the Indiana War Memorials Commission.*

Competing interests and changing priorities conspired to slow the process. From the outset, the idea of spending substantial resources on a grand memorial did not mesh well with the country's urgent need to help World War I veterans resettle into American society. Times were tough, and Indiana was about to spend $2.2 million on a war monument at a time when milk was $0.05 a gallon. The allocation of tax dollars to such an undertaking did not go without resistance or some resentment. The Great Depression and then the Second World War would draw additional attention and urgency from the project. But the obstacles most plain to see locally in the slow development of the memorial were those two churches anchoring the southeast and southwest corners of the memorial property.

THE TWO CHURCHES

The predicament surrounding the First Baptist and the Second Presbyterian Churches was perplexing. At one point in the original memorial plans for Square 16, it was agreed that the churches would be allowed to stay where they were and that the war memorial would be built on the block to the north. But the architects quickly decided the central shrine had to be constructed in the Square 16 block in order to harmonize their concept of the memorial as a whole. Its position between the houses of worship would poetically fulfill its ultimate mission—"For God and Country." But, ultimately, the designers argued that letting the churches stay in the block was "entirely illogical and out of keeping with the memorial." As the war memorial began to take shape, it became clear that the church buildings would obscure it, and the memorial would remain incomplete as long as it had to share the block with them.

When the architects insisted the commission renege on its original promise to let the churches stay, the churches asked them to reconsider, which resulted in a compromise: a 1925 law allowing the two churches on the site to remain there for twenty-five years. The designers weren't happy, but the issue remained relatively dormant for a number of years, largely the result of the economy and the war. And yet, as the years went on, the churches became as hamstrung by the arrangement as did the memorial itself. They were too hemmed in by the memorial to expand, and there was no chance of selling the properties, on a competitive basis, to anyone other than the memorial commission. The congregations suffered, and it had become more

A Walk along the Granite and the Limestone

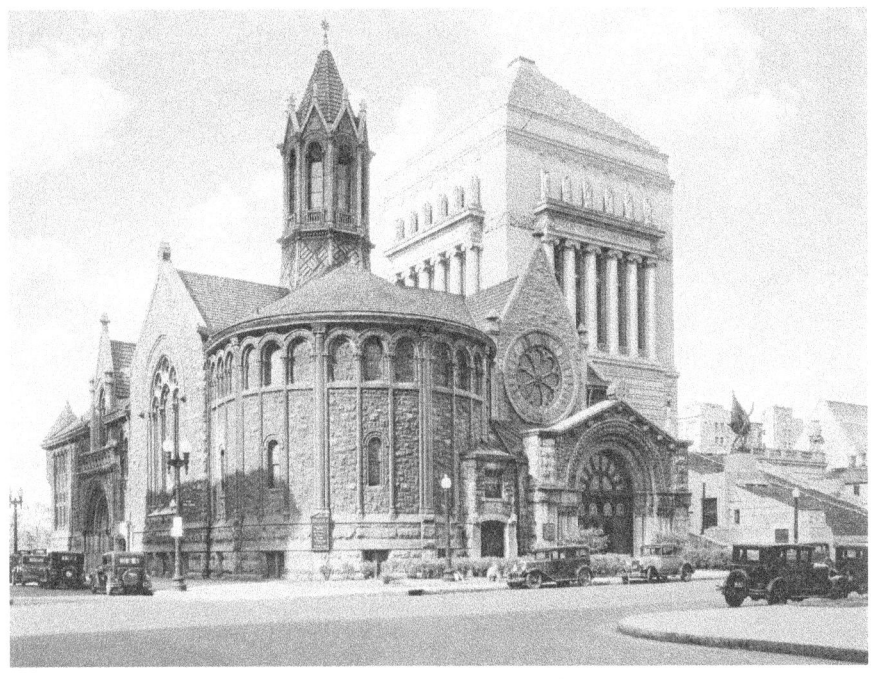

Above: First Baptist Church, at the corner of Vermont and Meridian Streets, as photographed in 1932, remains on the block after construction of the World War Memorial building. *Bass Photo Co. Collection, Indiana Historical Society.*

Left: Second Presbyterian Church at the corner of Vermont and Pennsylvania Streets, as photographed in 1932, remains on the block after construction of the World War Memorial building. *Bass Photo Co. Collection, Indiana Historical Society.*

and more difficult for the memorial and the churches to coexist. And so, as early as 1929, both the First Baptist Church and the Second Presbyterian Church indicated a willingness to negotiate.

Another reason to find a resolution to the church problem would have had a familiar ring. In 1920, the Indiana World War Memorial was a bargaining chip for Indianapolis in landing the American Legion headquarters. In 1945, *finishing* the memorial had become a checklist item in *keeping* it here.

But nothing was resolved until 1953, when the boards of both churches recommended cooperating with the memorial and the Indiana General Assembly created the World War Memorial Study Commission to consider, with more urgency, the feasibility of buying the church properties. In 1954,

Above: The view, looking to the southeast, of the new Indiana World War Memorial as it appeared in 1930, prior to the demolition of the First Baptist Church in the southwest corner of the block. *Bass Photo Co. Collection, Indiana Historical Society.*

Opposite, top: The view, looking north, of the Indiana World War Memorial and University Park from the Federal Building in 1930. The First Baptist and the Second Presbyterian Churches are visible to the left and right of the War Memorial. *Bass Photo Co. Collection, Indiana Historical Society.*

Opposite, bottom: The Indiana World War Memorial as it appeared in 1932. *Bass Photo Co. Collection, Indiana Historical Society.*

A Walk along the Granite and the Limestone

it recommended moving forward with the purchase, applying unused funds that had been raised for the memorial by a special tax levy enacted in 1945. The congregations sold their churches to be free at last of a predicament not of their making. And that meant the way would be clear for the completion of the setting and the exterior of the memorial.

No building in Square 16 survived the construction of the Indiana World War Memorial, but the First Baptist Church and the Second Presbyterian Church coexisted with it for thirty-five years. The Second Presbyterian Church finally moved out in 1959; the First Baptist Church, a year later. Not everyone, however, was pleased with the resolution of the conflict or the idea of those church buildings ultimately falling by the wayside in favor of the memorial. Frank Lloyd Wright visited the city in those days and remarked, "The churches on the Indiana World War Memorial Plaza should be left standing, and the architectural monstrosity of the war memorial torn down." But critique from the esteemed architect notwithstanding, both church buildings were razed in 1960, giving the

Close-up of the upper level of the Indiana World War Memorial, looking to the west, in 1953. *Bass Photo Co. Collection, Indiana Historical Society.*

A WALK ALONG THE GRANITE AND THE LIMESTONE

Undated postcard of the Indiana State World War Memorial. *Published by Kipp Brothers Co., Indianapolis, Indiana.*

city, for the first time, an unencumbered view of the memorial and room for filling in the landscaping and the missing pieces of the plaza on the southeast and southwest corners. The Indiana World War Memorial was finally completed, inside and out, in 1965.

A VIEW FROM THE STREET

From any direction, the Indiana World War Memorial still looks about the way it did in 1965. Only the details in the landscaping and the backdrops to the east and west of the memorial, particularly along Pennsylvania Street, have changed a little. The monument deserves a long moment of stopping and beholding from across the street, any street, because it honors the 135,000 Hoosiers who served in the Great War and the 3,000 who gave their lives to it, and because it is impressive and massive—the largest memorial to World War I anywhere in the nation.

The monument is built on a deep foundation of steel girders and reinforced concrete, rests appropriately on elevated ground and rises 210 feet above street level. Looking north and south, the base is 230 feet wide and 400 feet long. Its Neoclassical design, a theme uniting it with other structures along the mall, consistent with the City Beautiful Movement, recalls Greek architecture of the fifth century.

The towering square shrine structure designed by architects Frank B. Walker and Harry E. Weeks of Cleveland and sculpted by Henry Hering of New York is noted for its pyramidal dome, Ionic (scrolled) columns and formal, open spaces accented by heroic statuary. The origins of the architecture date back to 353 BCE and the construction of one of the seven wonders of the ancient world, an immense tomb built in the ancient city of Halicarnassus (modern-day Southwest Turkey) for King Mausolus of Persia. It was the first structure of its kind, a massive, decorated, freestanding building constructed as a monument, and it gave its name for what we now know as a mausoleum.

One of the most prominent features of the mausoleum-like Indiana World War Memorial is its distinctive ziggurat, a tower of pyramidal steps forming the roofline. Ziggurats were most characteristic of mausoleums in major cities in Mesopotamia (particularly present-day Iraq) and were seen as steps leading skyward, closer to heaven and the gods.

The war memorial, a temple of inspiring art and architecture encased in beautiful Indiana limestone, is crowned with an observation deck vaguely resembling a lantern but not intended as such. Watchmen were stationed on the observation deck during World War II. As implausible as it is in retrospect, they were charged with keeping an eye out for incoming German bombers.

Pro Patria

The view from University Park is a good place to begin a lap around the magnificent structure. While the main entrance to the Indiana World War Memorial is on the north side of the monument, it is the south side, the University Park side, that has *Pro Patria* perched on the steps welcoming visitors. Like the crowning figure on the Soldiers and Sailors Monument, he faces to the south.

When it was created, *Pro Patria* was the largest bronze casting ever sculpted in America. Standing proudly on a base of pink granite, the statue depicts a young man draped in an American flag reaching to the sky. Artist Henry Hering, who sculpted the seven-ton, twenty-four-foot-tall figure, helped explain the statue's significance: "I have attempted to embody in this memorial, the spirit rather than the material concept of the soldier—to give the figure an expression of all there is in humanity of

A Walk along the Granite and the Limestone

Pro Patria, facing south from the steps of the Indiana World War Memorial, ignores renovations to the memorial in the background, 2019. *Photo by Rudy Schouten.*

aspiration, valor, renunciation and the perpetuation of the memory of the patriot fighting for the right. I include peace also, for the left hand raised in exultation also may snatch the olive branch."

"Pro Patria" is a Latin phrase meaning "for country." The statue was set in place in 1929 and is the central sculptural element in the memorial's exterior.

The Tower Structure

The first tier of the monument, its wide base housing the visitor's center, rises about forty feet above street level to form a podium or "porch" surrounding the tower. This is the level at which the cornerstone was laid in 1927, in the northwest corner. A single, grand stairway rising directly from the sidewalk leads to the terrace roof from Vermont Street.

The tower itself is constructed in three levels: a lower section featuring rows of stone set in a distinct pattern, a larger section in the middle of the shaft with smoother limestone walls highlighted by sets of six magnificent stone columns and, finally, the pyramidal roof—the ziggurat, capped by its observation deck.

In the center section of the tower, on all four sides of the monument, five tall windows are nestled between the six columns. Above the stone columns stand six noble, heroic figures sculpted in stone. Characterized by their elegant simplicity, they represent, from left to right, courage, memory, peace, victory, liberty and patriotism. A frieze just below the figures surrounds the monument on all four sides.

The North Entrance
The only entrance to the monument is on the north side of the building. From the Michigan Street sidewalk, a set of low and wide granite and limestone stairways leads to four sets of bronze entry doors on the ground-floor level of the monument. To the right and the left, additional sets of stairways in two runs lead to the terrace level—the base of the tower.

Above the four entrance doors, an inscription quotes from the law creating the Indiana World War Memorial:

> *Erected to commemorate the valor and sacrifice of members of the land, sea and air forces of the United States and all others who rendered faithful and loyal service at home and overseas in the World War. To inculcate a true understanding and appreciation of the privileges of American citizenship. To inspire Patriotism and respect for the law to the end that Peace and good will may prevail, Justice be administered, Public Order maintained and Liberty perpetuated.*

A PEEK INSIDE

The Main Level
Beautiful marble floors and walls and an ornately beamed ceiling greet visitors stepping into the North Vestibule. For most, it's just the beginning of a revelation—three floors of inspiration and brilliant architectural surprises inside the familiar monolithic limestone exterior. The vestibule opens into the Grand Foyer, replete with more marble of varying colors and origins covering the floors, the walls and the columns—all under a segmented ceiling of richly decorated plaster.

The main floor features an Indiana 9/11 memorial, the "USS Indianapolis Memorial Highway" and an exhibit of the USS *Indianapolis* (CA35) Radio Room. It also houses administrative offices, exhibit space and meeting rooms in the form of Spruance and Shoup Halls, both elegant, seventy-five-seat facilities. Spruance Hall is named for Admiral Raymond A. Spruance, who commanded the USS *Indianapolis* throughout most of World War II, when it served as flagship of the Fifth Fleet in the Pacific. Spruance was raised in Indianapolis. The Shoup Room was named for David Monroe Shoup of Battle Ground, Indiana, who rose through the ranks to become a four-star marine general and commandant of the Marine Corps. The walls in the halls hold framed panels bearing the names of Indiana world war veterans who served in the navy; asterisks highlight the names of those who perished.

But the main attraction on this floor is the gorgeous, five-hundred-seat Pershing Auditorium, situated precisely in the center of the building. In addition to its vivid architectural detail, including trim of American red marble, the walls and the ceiling of this room were constructed with distinctive Guastavino acoustic tile, a focus on sound quality well ahead of its time. The first public performance in the new auditorium, which took place on April 4, 1937 (before the official dedication of the building), was a piano recital by Sara Miller, a member of the faculty of the Arthur Jordan Conservatory of Music. A local newspaper review described the impressive setting: "Its strikingly attractive stage, its highly polished pillars and panels of variegated brown marble, its comfortable plush seats and its excellent acoustical treatment will make it a highly popular meeting place for musical audiences of 600 or less for many years to come."

The front entrance to the Pershing Auditorium is through the Grand Foyer, but the room is also accessible by way of the East and West Vestibules of the main floor.

The Shrine Room
On either side of the Grand Foyer entrance to the Pershing Auditorium stand elegant marble arches framing the way to two grand staircases. They ascend to the Shrine Room, directly above the auditorium. The stairways, works of art in themselves, bear wall panels displaying the names of Indiana world war veterans who served in the U.S. Army and the Marine Corps. Those who died in the service of their country are noted.

The climb up the stairs is one to be taken slowly and in due reverence to the men and women listed. And the room to which it leads is a fitting place for contemplating their sacrifices. The Shrine Room, dedicated on Armistice Day, November 11, 1933, by Lieutenant General Hugh Drum, deputy chief of staff of the United States Army, and Governor Paul McNutt, is the "emotional and architectural core of the memorial." Its purpose, simply, is to "inspire citizenship amongst all who visit."

The Shrine Room is full of symbolism, beginning with its construction of material from all over the world, representing the global nature of the "Great War." The room soars to 110 feet and is 60 feet square. Hanging high above from the center of the room is the Star of Destiny, a huge Swedish crystal fixture offering light to "guide the welfare of the nation."

Hanging heroically below the star is a giant American flag. And at floor level, below the garrison flag surrounded by sentinel torches, rests the Altar of Consecration—the altar to the flag, "a place for honoring fallen soldiers and comrades."

Royal Cortissoz, an American art historian who wrote the inscription on the Lincoln Memorial, also wrote the words inscribed on the four sides of the altar, a call of fellowship to the nations of the world.

> *North:* "*In the stars of our flag shines the steadfastness of the stars in heaven, they light the paths of men to courage, devotion and patriotism.*"
> *South:* "*Within this shrine there lives the spirit of brotherhood binding the people of the United States with the nations of the world.*"
> *East:* "*The true patriot best supports his government by creating friendliness through kindness and generosity wherever fate may carry him.*"
> *West:* "*Valor is needed in peace to sustain the unending war for truth and beauty which enrich life while they fortify against adversity.*"

The Star of Destiny, the flag and the altar are the heart of the Shrine Room's purpose, but it is the room itself—its architecture, its shape, its colors and its lighting—that creates the emotion and the inspiration of the place.

The room's perimeter is lined with forty-foot columns made of red marble from Vermont—blood-red marble meant to symbolize the blood shed during World War I. The columns are placed closely together not only to support its vast ceiling but also to represent that which was essential in defending the nation. Alcoves formed by the columns on the east and west ends of the room frame Walter Brough portraits of the military commanders of the six leading Allied forces in the war: the United States, France, England, Belgium, Italy and Serbia.

An allegorical marble frieze sculpted by Frank Jirouch represents, on the north wall, America joining the Allied forces in World War I; on the east and west walls, images of the great struggle; and on the south wall, the portrayal of a contrasting ultimate peace.

Unique lighting and twenty tall, elegant stained-glass windows above the frieze, five on each side of the room, help imbue the space with inspirational tones of blue representing freedom, the American armed forces and the American flag as well as the flags hanging there in tribute to fellow nations that served the Allied cause. This temple is not just a memorial to our heroes but also a call for world peace and unity.

The Museum

The setting and the emotion of the Shrine Room are unmistakable; so it isn't surprising that visitors leave it with a renewed sense of patriotism and a greater appreciation for the sacrifices made by those who fought in the "Great War." And as they walk back down the grand staircase to the main level, and then a few more steps down to a lower level on the south side of the memorial, a collection of the more tangible reminders of the history and the conduct of war await them in the Indiana World War Memorial Museum.

The military museum is 30,000 square feet of exhibit space illustrating Indiana's history of participation in every American conflict, from the Battle of Tippecanoe to the present. Highlights include the USS *Indianapolis* (CA-35) Gallery, a Vietnam-era Cobra helicopter, the commission plate of the battleship USS *Indiana* (BB-58) and hundreds of displays featuring military photos, artifacts, documents, firearms and uniforms. The Indiana World War Memorial also houses the Colonel Eli Lilly Civil War Museum and a display of artifacts from the Civil War and the Spanish-American War.

STOP 4
VETERANS MEMORIAL PLAZA

SOLEMN GROUNDS

The second block in the city's 1920 blueprint for the war memorial monument was Square 5, which is the block immediately north of the Indiana War Memorial. It also sets the northern boundary of the Mile Square. Square 5 is the present-day Veteran's Memorial Plaza, the middle lot in the larger five-block tract designated as the Indiana World War Memorial Plaza. It was set aside to honor all Indiana veterans, create a gathering place within the mall and, through its landscape architecture, add grandeur to the setting of the shrine, the war memorial building itself.

MORE SACRIFICES

But like the block to the south hosting the shrine, Square 5 had significant structures standing in the way of its new purpose. A 1921 newspaper account diagrammed twenty-nine structures slated for demolition, a blend of stately old homes, upscale apartment buildings and businesses that had begun to encroach into the residential setting.

Of the twenty-nine buildings on the block at the time, twenty were houses or apartments. The north side of Michigan Street was perhaps the best

A Walk along the Granite and the Limestone

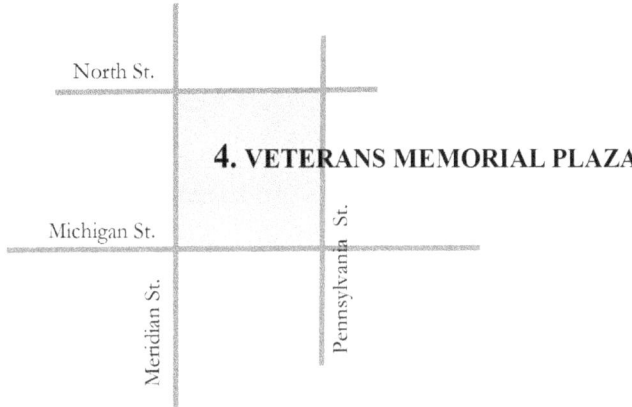

Map segment of Veterans Memorial Plaza. *Map by Rudy Schouten.*

The Chalfant Flat Apartment Building at 20 East Michigan Street, the corner of Michigan and Pennsylvania Streets, as it appeared in 1907. *Bass Photo Co. Collection, Indiana Historical Society.*

The Historic Memorial District of Downtown Indianapolis

remaining illustration of the residential quality that once characterized the area. The stretch of Michigan from Meridian to Pennsylvania Streets still included five brick and stone homes, the San-Toy Flats and the Chalfant Apartments at the corner of Michigan and Pennsylvania Streets.

John Chalfant New, a local notable in financial and political circles who went on to serve as chairman of the Republican Party and treasurer of the United States, had the Chalfant Apartments built in 1896. It housed the American Legion and hosted its executive committee meetings during construction of the memorial. But the committee members would be among the building's final tenants; the Chalfant was demolished in 1925. John C. New's personal home was located just down the street from the Chalfant at 518 North Pennsylvania Street, where it hosted a long list of prominent citizens, including James Whitcomb Riley, and enjoyed the rare distinction of being owned and occupied by the same family, the New family, for its entire existence—from its construction in 1873 until the war memorial claimed the property in 1922.

Additional residences were scattered throughout the block, including some fronting the interior alleys; the Hotel Altenburg (originally the Charleston

Street scene of brick houses looking south along Pennsylvania Street, circa 1915. The Chalfant Apartments appear on the far left, at the intersection of Pennsylvania and Michigan Streets. The John Chalfant New home is the third from the right. *Bass Photo Co. Collection, Indiana Historical Society.*

A Walk along the Granite and the Limestone

The Propylaeum on North Street as it appeared in 1917. *Bass Photo Co. Collection, Indiana Historical Society.*

Inn) faced Meridian Street. On the northeast quadrant, businesses dominated, with a printing company, a tailor, a photographer, an undertaker and Crawford Drugs on the corner. But the most distinguished structure on the block was the Propylaeum at 17 East North Street.

The Indianapolis Woman's Club founded the Propylaeum in 1888 "for the purpose of promoting and encouraging literary and scientific endeavors, also for erecting and maintaining a suitable building that would provide a center of higher culture for the public, and particularly for the women of Indianapolis." They chose to build it on North Street for its central location in Indianapolis, its easy access to streetcars and its attractive setting—fronting the grounds of the Institution for the Blind across the street to the north, another landmark structure that would eventually yield to the memorial.

Propylaeum, a Greek term for the architecture of a porch or gatehouse at the entrance of a sacred enclosure, was fitting for the impressive structure of brick, iron and limestone. The Propylaeum, whose cornerstone was laid in 1890, was dedicated in 1891. It was razed in 1923. At that point, the club relocated to the former Schaf-Schmidt house at 1410 North Delaware Street, where it remains today.

THE HISTORIC MEMORIAL DISTRICT OF DOWNTOWN INDIANAPOLIS

A TRANSFORMATION

When Square 5 was finally cleared of the likes of the Chalfant and the Propylaeum in the 1920s, the block quickly assumed a dramatically new look and a new mission, and neither has changed very much since then.

The focal point for the new space honoring Indiana veterans would be an obelisk surrounded by a fountain in the center of the square. It was thus known originally, and for some to this day, as Obelisk Square. Under the direction of architectural sculptor Henry Hering, construction of the obelisk began in 1923, just two years after preliminary work had begun on the Indiana World War Memorial. The obelisk and the square were completed in 1930, and soon after that, the ground was paved for use by large groups

Above: Work begins on Block No. 5 of the Indiana World War Memorial Plaza, Obelisk Square, October 1, 1928. *Photo courtesy of the Indiana War Memorials Commission.*

Opposite, top: Construction of the obelisk in the Indiana War Memorial Plaza is well underway, March 11, 1929. To the left, in the background, is the Indianapolis Scottish Rite Cathedral; and to the right, the Indiana School for the Blind. *Photo courtesy of the Indiana War Memorials Commission.*

Opposite, bottom: Obelisk Square under construction in Veterans Memorial Plaza in 1923, with Scottish Rite Cathedral and the Indiana School for the Blind in the background. *Bass Photo Co. Collection, Indiana Historical Society.*

A Walk along the Granite and the Limestone

The Historic Memorial District of Downtown Indianapolis

Workers apply finishing touches to the obelisk in the Indiana War Memorial Plaza. *Photo courtesy of the Indiana War Memorials Commission.*

gathering there to listen to bands or watch the colored lights in the fountains. The outside corners of the square featured displays of heavy artillery—World War I tanks and cannons.

Obelisk Square seemed a little worn, untidy and unfriendly by the time it approached fifty years of service in the mid-1970s. The coming bicentennial applied additional pressure on the city and the state to consider

Above: Obelisk Square looking to the southeast in 1936, with War Memorial in the background. *Bass Photo Co. Collection, Indiana Historical Society.*

Right: Obelisk and fountain as they appeared in 1950, still surrounded by pavement. The Hotel English in the background was the new home of the old English Hotel and Opera House on Monument Circle, which was torn down two years earlier. *Bass Photo Co. Collection, Indiana Historical Society.*

The Historic Memorial District of Downtown Indianapolis

Postcard showing "Obelisk Square" (now Veterans Memorial Plaza) in the late 1970s, after a beautification of the square. *Photo by McGuire Studio and Indiana Scenic Images, Indianapolis.*

upgrades to the public space, so, in August 1975, Governor Otis Bowen announced plans for a long-awaited beautification of Obelisk Square. The *Indianapolis Star* reported that it would "transform the square-block area from a barren field of asphalt and weeds into a downtown haven of trees and a flowing fountain of flags."

In the coming months, the obelisk and the fountain were fully restored, faulty underground plumbing for the fountain was repaired and new lighting was installed. Most of the dominant ground cover in Obelisk Square, wide swaths of concrete and asphalt where tanks and cannons once stood, was replaced with grass, trees and a formal pattern of walkways inside the square. A terrace of fifty state flags and the American flag, the Bicentennial Terrace, was added to the north side of square, symbolizing "the spirit of individualism and unity characterizing a democratic society." By the time the bicentennial rolled around in 1976, Obelisk Square, now Veterans Memorial Plaza, had been transformed into something much brighter and much more like an urban park setting.

A CLOSER LOOK

The obelisk, the highlight of Veterans Memorial Plaza from any angle, is a four-sided shaft of black Berwick granite standing one hundred feet tall and capped in a pinnacle of gold leaf. The obelisk itself is a symbol of regeneration, representing "the hopes and aspirations of the nation, a symbol of the power of nature to reproduce and continue the life of the country." At the base of the obelisk, four four-by-eight-foot bronze bas-relief tablets, one on each side, represent "the four fundamentals on which the nation's hopes are founded: *Law, Science, Religion,* and *Education.*"

Encircling the obelisk, the two-level fountain is made of pink Georgia marble and terrazzo. The lower basin is a perfect circle one hundred feet wide, and the upper basin is divided into four smaller, semicircular bays. High jet sprays, one in each of the upper bays, is accented by a ring of smaller jets in the lower basin. In keeping with the original design and operation of the fountain, multicolored lighting adds ambiance to the setting at night.

The obelisk and fountain in Veterans Memorial Plaza with the Indianapolis Scottish Rite Cathedral in the background. *Photo by Rudy Schouten, 2019.*

The Historic Memorial District of Downtown Indianapolis

Right: One of the four panels at the base of the obelisk. *Photo by Rudy Schouten.*

Below: One of two flag terraces, east and west of the obelisk, in Veterans Memorial Plaza. *Photo by Rudy Schouten.*

Veterans Memorial Plaza was reconfigured again in 2004, although not as dramatically as it had been in 1975. New landscaping and lawn spaces were added to the north and south ends of the plaza, lighting was upgraded and crumbling sidewalks were replaced. In 2005, the fifty flags that had anchored the north end of the plaza were divided into two separate terraces of twenty-five state flags and relocated to the east and west edges of the block. As with previous upgrades, the changes were part of an effort to make way for uninterrupted north–south views from the Central Library to the Indiana World War Memorial. Each of the two terraces is accompanied by a single American flag, and the state flags are arranged in the order in which the states entered the union.

STOP 5
AMERICAN LEGION MALL

AN HONORED OPPORTUNITY

The spirit and the culture behind the war memorials of Indianapolis were established before the turn of the twentieth century, when the inspiration for a Civil War monument took hold and a purely civic purpose was slowly wrenched out of other plans for University Square. But the driving force behind Indiana War Memorial Plaza was the American Legion. The aesthetic vision for the plaza and its development fell into place quickly when the city landed the Legion's national headquarters and saw a canvas for it. Ground-breaking for the Indiana World War Memorial, Veterans Memorial Plaza and the American Legion headquarters all took place within a four-year time frame.

The land set aside by the Indiana General Assembly "to provide a suitable building for the National Headquarters of the American Legion" consisted of the two blocks between North Street, the northern edge of Veterans Memorial Plaza, and St. Clair Street—a neat fit and an appropriate setting in the axis of memorials between the U.S. Courthouse and the public library. Like other city squares in the war memorial property, the footprint for the proposed American Legion, the first two city blocks north of the Mile Square between Meridian and Pennsylvania Streets, had some old history to clear away before development could begin.

A WALK ALONG THE GRANITE AND THE LIMESTONE

Map segment of American Legion Mall. *Map by Rudy Schouten.*

BEFORE THE LEGION

In 1845, the Indiana General Assembly appropriated $5,000 to buy land needed for building a school for the blind, eventually selecting an eight-acre site on North Street between Meridian and Pennsylvania Streets. Three years later, another $5,000 was set aside to begin the work. Temporary quarters were built for managing immediate needs before construction of a permanent building was begun in 1850 and completed in 1853; it was the Indiana School for the Blind, the grand structure across the street from the old Propylaeum.

The school commanded a distinguished setting in the city's outer reaches, occupying the entire two-block area that would be claimed for the American Legion Mall. But the grounds for the Indiana School for the Blind were scaled back before 1900, when the block to the north was designated as St. Clair Park.

The five-story, brick-and-sandstone building was designed by Hoosier architect Francis Costigan, who was also noted for his work on historic buildings in Madison, Indiana. The school boasted two four-story wings, Ionic portico and verandas, four large stone scrolls lining the wide main entry staircase and three distinctive cupolas gracing the rooftops, only one of which survived into the 1920s. The property, surrounded by an iron fence, also included dormitories, a barn, a workshop, a laundry, a bakeshop and a

The Historic Memorial District of Downtown Indianapolis

The Indiana School for the Blind on North Street as it appeared in 1903. *Bass Photo Co. Collection, Indiana Historical Society.*

The Indiana School for the Blind on North Street, looking to the northeast, as it appeared in 1928. *Bass Photo Co. Collection, Indiana Historical Society.*

A Walk along the Granite and the Limestone

The Indiana School for the Blind in 1928, with the Scottish Rite Cathedral under construction to the left. The construction site for Veterans Memorial Plaza is in the foreground, and the St. Clair Street Marion Co. Library is visible behind the school for the blind to the right. *Bass Photo Co. Collection, Indiana Historical Society.*

The Indiana School for the Blind in 1929, showing detail of south entryway and Scottish Rite Cathedral, tower construction now complete, in the background. *Bass Photo Co. Collection, Indiana Historical Society.*

The Historic Memorial District of Downtown Indianapolis

The Indiana School for the Blind, looking to the northeast from Meridian Street, in 1930, with a corner of the completed Veterans Memorial Plaza in the foreground. *Bass Photo Co. Collection, Indiana Historical Society.*

greenhouse. The $5,000 appropriation was a start, but the complex—the buildings and the grounds—would eventually cost $110,000 to build.

When the state authorized the development of the Indiana World War Memorial Plaza, it also approved a plan for a new school for the blind at Seventy-Fifth Street and North College Avenue; the old one had to go. In 1930, the Indiana School for the Blind building on North Street was razed, just one among the forty-five buildings in the five-block plaza yielding to the memorial.

THE LEGION RISES

Plans for the American Legion Mall started, wisely, with the needs of the Legion itself. In 1923, architects presented the memorial commission with its proposal:

A Walk along the Granite and the Limestone

Two office buildings will constitute the utilitarian part of the memorial. They will be in St. Clair Park. The buildings, almost identical in exterior appearance, will extend lengthwise north and south along Pennsylvania and Meridian Streets. They will be four stories in height with the fourth story set back so that it will not be in view from the street. The buildings will harmonize with the library building. They will cost about $250,000 apiece.

Ground was broken for the American Legion National Headquarters at Meridian and St. Clair Streets (the northwest corner of St. Clair Park) in June 1924. Mayor Shank proclaimed, "We break ground on a project that will make Indianapolis the patriotic shrine of America." When construction work was finished in 1925, it was the first new structure on the mall. But the second of the two buildings, as originally proposed for the northeast corner of the park, would not be built until 1950, when the Legion outgrew the first. When the American Legion National Headquarters moved into its more spacious building across the mall, the American Legion's Indiana headquarters moved into the original structure.

Construction underway on American Legion Building "B" on Meridian Street, October 27, 1924. *Photo courtesy of the Indiana War Memorials Commission.*

The Historic Memorial District of Downtown Indianapolis

American Legion National Headquarters, 1925. A portion of the back of the Indiana Blind School, still standing in 1925, appears on the right. *Bass Photo Co. Collection, Indiana Historical Society.*

Landscaping and development of American Legion Mall, July 27, 1931. *Photo courtesy of the Indiana War Memorials Commission.*

A Walk along the Granite and the Limestone

Foundation work on the new American Legion Building (Unit "C") on Pennsylvania Street, November 18, 1948. *Photo courtesy of the Indiana War Memorials Commission.*

Progress on construction of the new American Legion Building, May 19, 1949. In the background, across the mall, stands the original American Legion building, and to the right is the Marion County Library. *Photo courtesy of the Indiana War Memorials Commission.*

The Historic Memorial District of Downtown Indianapolis

Above: The American Legion National Headquarters, facing Pennsylvania Street, in 1951. *Bass Photo Co. Collection, Indiana Historical Society.*

Left: Entrance to American Legion National Headquarters from inside the mall, 1951. *Bass Photo Co. Collection, Indiana Historical Society.*

Construction of the centerpiece of the American Legion Mall, the sunken garden and Cenotaph Square, began in 1930, just weeks after the school for the blind was demolished. The cenotaph, which cost an estimated $75,000 to build, was dedicated on Veterans Day of 1932. Paul McNutt and Raymond Springer, both past state commanders of the American Legion and candidates for governor that year, presided over the festivities.

But it would take another sixty-five years for the mall to look like it does today. In 1950, when the Legion opened its ranks to veterans of World War II, the State of Indiana built the new American Legion National Headquarters, nearly twice the size of the original, and the mall itself underwent years of modifications to the landscape design and, in the late 1990s, the addition of the Vietnam, Korean and World War II memorials.

A STROLL THROUGH THE MALL

The American Legion Mall is distinguished by the sunken grassy grounds stretching nearly the length of its two-block footprint, an open expanse setting the stage for the cenotaph in the center on the north end. Stairways on all four sides of the mall lead to the sunken garden and the cenotaph; all other structures on the mall are set at street level.

The Korean and Vietnam Memorials

From Veterans Memorial Plaza, crossing North Street into American Legion Mall, visitors will find contemporary, nearly identical war memorials in the southeast and southwest corners. These limestone and granite memorials honor those who served in the Korean and Vietnam Wars. Both were designed by architect Patrick Brunner and dedicated during Memorial Day services in 1996.

The memorials are both twenty-five feet tall and shaped as segments of a cylinder twelve and a half feet in diameter. The names of the men and women killed in the conflicts are inscribed on the concave side of the monuments—927 in Korea and 1,525 in Vietnam. On the convex sides, which face the streets, inscriptions include narrative on the conduct of the wars and excerpts from letters written by troops from the battlefield.

The Historic Memorial District of Downtown Indianapolis

Korean War Memorial, American Legion Mall, 2019. *Photo by Rudy Schouten.*

Vietnam War Memorial, American Legion Mall, 2019. *Photo by Rudy Schouten.*

The World War II Memorial

The World War II Memorial, which stands a little north of the Korean Memorial on the east side of the mall, was designed to be very similar to the Korean and Vietnam War Memorials but is larger, to represent the war's relative size and scale. World War II claimed almost twelve thousand Hoosier lives, and another seventeen thousand Indiana men and women were wounded. This memorial, also designed by Patrick Brunner, is the most recent addition to American Legion Mall. Senator Bob Dole, national chairman of the World War II Memorial Campaign, delivered the keynote address at its dedication on Memorial Day in 1998. Dole had been a platoon leader in the legendary Tenth Mountain Division in Italy during the war and was gravely wounded on the battlefield in 1945. He was decorated twice for his heroism.

The half-circle granite and limestone monument is just less than twenty feet wide and has a radius of nine feet, 2 inches. The concave side has excerpts from letters written by Indiana World War II veterans. A freestanding column lists the order of the war's campaigns and operations. The convex side, which faces the street, is inscribed with the story of the war and a listing of notable Indiana units and Hoosier Medal of Honor recipients.

World War II Memorial, American Legion Mall, 2019. *Photo by Rudy Schouten*.

The Historic Memorial District of Downtown Indianapolis

The American Legion National Headquarters

Just north of the World War II Memorial, fronting Pennsylvania Street, is the American Legion National Headquarters, essentially the reason the mall and the plaza exist. Very much in keeping with the originally proposed designs and the existing architecture along the plaza, this Neoclassical structure was built in 1950 to serve the expanding needs of the Legion. The building has four stories, with its top floor set back so as not to be seen easily from the street. It is designed with two wings connected by a recessed center section and an entrance framed by Doric columns supporting a full entablature.

What goes on inside is a reflection of the American Legion's "Four Pillars": "Veterans Affairs & Rehabilitation, National Security, Americanism, and Children & Youth." The fourth floor, the space featured in public tours of the facility, includes a library and archives that hold printed material on the American Legion's history and a complete, indexed collection of the *American Legion Magazine*, the world's most-read publication for veterans. The Emil A. Blackmore Museum, which was opened in 1967 and named for the U.S. Navy veteran of World War II who served as the seventh national adjutant of the American Legion, showcases the history of the Legion and the wars in which Legion members have fought. Museum exhibits include American Legion uniforms, badges, medals and other memorabilia.

Other highlights on the fourth floor include the Fine Arts Gallery, an American Legion collection of paintings, sculptures, prints and photographs created in honor of the service of American veterans, and the NEC Room, an elegant hall used by the Legion's National Executive Committee. The NEC is the Legion's governing body between national conventions. The Legion's fifty-five departments gather in the room twice a year; each department, by tradition, has its own desk. The room also features noteworthy paintings of the signing of the German surrender at the end of World War II in Reims, France, and the signing of the Japanese surrender on board the battleship USS *Missouri* in Tokyo Bay.

The third floor of the American Legion building houses executive offices for the national commander (a new commander is elected every year) and the Finance and Internal Affairs Divisions. The Endowment Room hosts the American Legion Endowment Fund Corporation, which meets there to discuss investments that provide funding for Veterans Affairs & Rehabilitation and Children & Youth programs. A memorial in the room honors Harry W. Colmery, a past national commander perhaps best known as the "architect of the GI Bill of Rights."

A WALK ALONG THE GRANITE AND THE LIMESTONE

Postcard showing the American Legion National Headquarters, built in 1950. *Published by Van Buren Color, Indianapolis, Indiana.*

The second floor is headquarters for the Citizens Flag Alliance, a group organized by the American Legion in 1994 to persuade Congress to restore the American people's right to protect the flag. The floor also houses offices for the Information Technology Division, the Media Division and the Americanism and Children & Youth Division, which, among many other things, coordinates and administers American Legion Baseball, the National High School Oratorical Contest, Boy Scouts and American Legion scholarships. And on the first floor, among a collection of original World War I and World War II recruiting posters decorating the walls, are offices busy with the work of providing additional support services—purchasing, document processing, human resources, marketing and convention planning.

The American Legion, Indiana Headquarters
The smaller twin brother to the American Legion National Headquarters building stands directly across the mall along Meridian Street and served as the design model for the bigger version. It is the oldest building on the plaza and the first permanent home of the American Legion. When construction work began, the Indiana War Memorial was known as "Building A," this

The Historic Memorial District of Downtown Indianapolis

Postcard showing the original American Legion National Headquarters, built in 1925. Published by *Kipp Brothers Co., Indianapolis, Indiana.*

structure (the original American Legion building) was "Building B" and the National American Legion building along Pennsylvania Street was known as "Unit C."

Cenotaph Square

Cenotaph Square, which is the most solemn location on the properties, was built to pay tribute to Hoosiers who have died in war. It rests elegantly on the north end of the sunken garden, midway between the two American Legion buildings. This memorial was originally planned as a tomb for the remains of Corporal James Bethel Gresham of Evansville, Indiana, who was the nation's first combat death of the Great War. But despite the memorial commission's best efforts to move Gresham's final resting place to Indianapolis, his parents were sure they wanted their son to remain buried near his home. As a result, it was determined that the memorial would be completed as a cenotaph, an empty tomb or monument erected in honor of a person who is buried elsewhere. It would remain empty and be dedicated to all the dead of World War I.

The raised rectangular cenotaph is made of black granite. It rests on a low platform of green and red granite which is set on a floor of polished red and green granite squares. A bronze wreath is embedded in the floor on three

A Walk along the Granite and the Limestone

Aerial view, looking north, of American Legion Mall in 1932, illustrating its original landscape design. *Bass Photo Co. Collection, Indiana Historical Society.*

The cenotaph and American Legion Mall in 1935, after completion of the original national headquarters but before construction of the larger headquarters across the mall. *Bass Photo Co. Collection, Indiana Historical Society.*

The Historic Memorial District of Downtown Indianapolis

Cenotaph Square in its sunken garden, looking to the north, with the Marion County Library in the background, in 1946. *Bass Photo Co. Collection, Indiana Historical Society.*

The obelisk in Veterans Memorial Plaza and the American Legion Mall, looking to the north, in 1953, after completion of the new American Legion National Headquarters on Pennsylvania Street. *Bass Photo Co. Collection, Indiana Historical Society.*

A Walk along the Granite and the Limestone

Postcard, dated 1959, showing Cenotaph Square and the American Legion National Headquarters. *Distributed by Koch News Co., Indianapolis, Indiana.*

Cenotaph in American Legion Mall with the original American Legion Building in the background, 2018. *Photo by Rudy Schouten.*

The Historic Memorial District of Downtown Indianapolis

The cenotaph, looking south into the American Legion Mall, 2018. *Photo by Rudy Schouten.*

sides, and a bronze plaque on the north side of the cenotaph memorializes Gresham: "In Memoriam, James Bethel Gresham of Evansville, IN, Corporal, Co. F, 16th Infantry, 1st Division, A.E.F. Killed at Bathelmont, France, Nov. 3, 1917. First member of American Expeditionary Forces to lose his life in action in the World War, 1917–1918."

Inscriptions on the north and south panels of the tomb read: "A tribute by Indiana to the hallowed memory of the glorious dead who served in the World War." The cenotaph is guarded at each corner by black granite columns crowned by bronze American eagles plated in gold.

Part IV

THE CANAL MEMORIALS

While the core of the holdings of the Indiana War Memorials Commission consists of the monuments and memorials along Meridian Street, the commission also manages three significant, more contemporary memorials along the Indianapolis Central Canal, all just a few short blocks from the historic district.

But the Central Canal has a rich history, too. As it turns out, it never served the purpose intended for it when it was proposed and developed in the late 1830s. The nine miles of it completed by the time the project was abandoned would never be the central Indiana link to commercial traffic envisioned by Alexander Ralston and the city planners. And any urgency in returning to the work at a later date faded with the development of the railroad system in central Indiana. Instead, nature took over to make a more recreational setting of the canal. A towpath along the route served to expedite local commerce, but the canal also developed as a popular destination for hikers and fishermen as well as a great setting for a pleasant walk or bike ride along the water.

Public use of the canal didn't change all that much when the state sold it to private investors in 1851 or when it was sold to the Indianapolis Hydraulic Company, a predecessor of the Indianapolis Water Company, in 1869. At that time, however, the canal entered a new era and began to take on the additional role of transporting water for the Indianapolis water utility, which continued to use the downtown portion of the canal for its waterworks operation into the 1960s.

The Historic Memorial District of Downtown Indianapolis

*The Indianapolis
Central Canal Memorials*

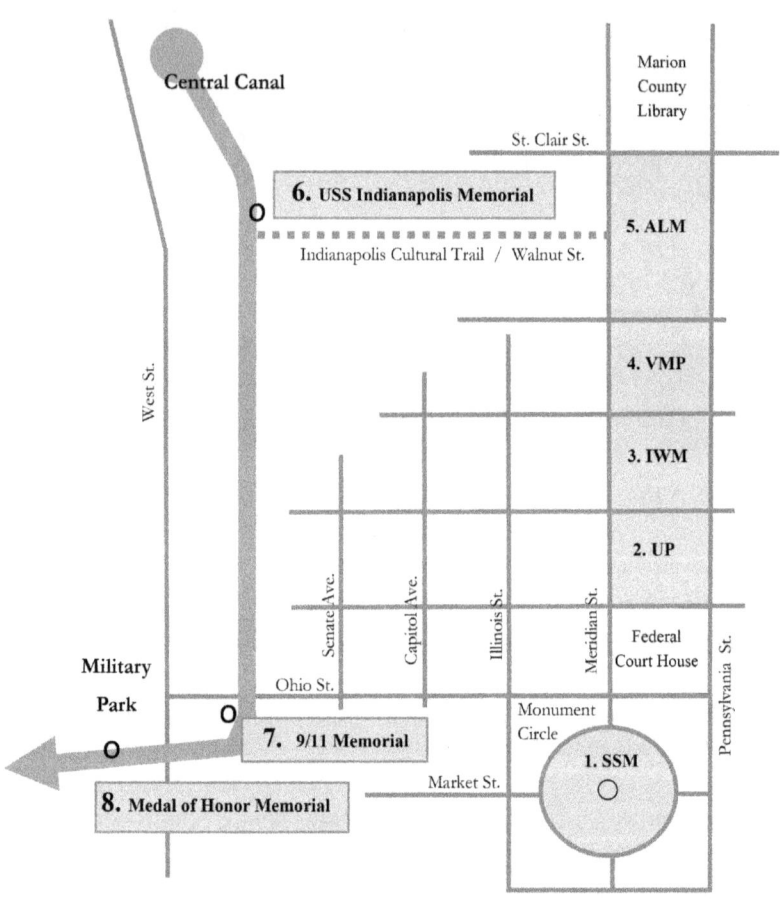

Map of the three Canal Memorials and the route to the canal from American Legion Mall.
Map by Rudy Schouten.

The Canal Memorials

But the character of the area surrounding the canal changed over time, and it had long since lost its recreational appeal when, in 1979, the Indiana General Assembly created the White River State Park Development Commission. Its mission was to develop a plan for reviving the near west side of downtown Indianapolis, an area, by the way, centered on the spot where Governor Jennings's state commission convened in 1820 to select a new state capital—settler John McCormick's cabin.

Within a few short years, the city embarked on a plan to refurbish the old dirt-bottomed canal and redevelop its immediate surroundings as part of the White River State Park project. The downtown canal beautification campaign of the 1980s included work on the Indiana Government Center and the State Garage, and a renovation of the statehouse for the building's centennial. The larger vicinity bounded by New York, North, West and Illinois Streets would be transformed into a new residential, commercial and business community. The canal was the center amenity in the development. All of it set the stage for additional projects in the complex—the Indianapolis Zoo, the Eiteljorg Museum, the Washington Street bridge walkway connecting the attractions, Victory Field, the NCAA Hall of Champions, the new Indiana State Museum and a 1,760-foot extension of the new Central Canal, historically significant because it followed a westward portion of the original waterway.

While a dirt towpath had no role in the new version of the Central Canal, wide, paved walkways certainly did. And today, among the attractions available to strollers on the scenic Canal Walk are those three additional memorials.

STOP 6
THE USS *INDIANAPOLIS* CA35 NATIONAL MEMORIAL

Starting from American Legion Mall, a three-block walk west on the Walnut Street segment of the Indianapolis Cultural Trail leads directly to the USS Indianapolis CA35 Memorial, a national monument on the east bank of Indy's Central Canal.

The USS *Indianapolis*, a heavy cruiser distinguished for its service with ten battle stars, had just completed a secret mission to Tinian Island, one of three islands in the Northern Marianas, about fifteen hundred miles south of Tokyo, where it delivered the components of the world's first

The USS *Indianapolis* CA35 Memorial on the Central Canal Walk, 2019. *Photo by Rudy Schouten.*

operational atomic bombs. It then continued on to Guam for new orders, which were to join, without an escort, an assembling invasion fleet at Leyte Gulf in the Philippines. On July 30, 1945, about halfway between Guam and Leyte, the USS *Indianapolis* was struck by two torpedoes fired by a submarine of the Imperial Japanese Navy. Of the 1,195 U.S. sailors on board, only 316 survived.

Designed by Indianapolis architect Joseph Fischer, the USS Indianapolis CA35 National Memorial was dedicated in 1995 to recognize those who served on the last U.S. ship to sink during World War II. The memorial is the result of a thirty-five-year effort by the survivors to build a fitting tribute to their lost shipmates. The twenty-one-ton memorial of gray and black granite is sculpted in the shape of the ship and is etched on one side with the story of the sinking and on the other with the names of those on the Final Sailing List.

STOP 7
THE INDIANA 9/11 MEMORIAL

Follow the Canal Walk south about five blocks to find the Indiana 9/11 Memorial, situated just west of the canal along the south side of Ohio Street. The Indiana 9/11 Memorial was established in 2010 to honor those who perished in the attacks.

The memorial is made up of two black granite walls, each six feet tall and inscribed with recollections of the events on that day in New York City, Washington, D.C., and Shanksville, Pennsylvania. Rising in front of the granite walls are two eleven-thousand-pound beams recovered from

The Indiana 9/11 Memorial on the Central Canal Walk, 2019. *Photo by Rudy Schouten.*

the wreckage of the Twin Towers. They didn't arrive in Indianapolis to take their place in the memorial without considerable effort. Greg Hess, an Indianapolis firefighter and a member of one of the first Federal Emergency Management Agency teams, Indiana Task Force One, to arrive in New York (within hours of the attacks), spent years petitioning officials in New York for the honor of bringing those beams home to the city. One of the beams is topped with a life-sized bronze sculpture of an American bald eagle looking east in the direction of New York City.

STOP 8
THE MEDAL OF HONOR MEMORIAL

The Medal of Honor Memorial, a national monument, can be found just around the corner from the Indiana 9/11 Memorial by continuing along the Canal Walk as it bends past West Street to the southern edge of Military Park. Military Park, yet another popular setting for city festivals and patriotic gatherings, was once a Civil War encampment and, later, the location of Indiana's first state fair. The Medal of Honor Memorial, the nation's first memorial honoring all recipients

The Medal of Honor Memorial on the Central Canal Walk, 2019. *Photo by Rudy Schouten.*

of its highest award for military valor, was inspired by John Hodowal, chairman of the Indianapolis Power and Light Company Foundation, and his wife, Caroline. It was created by artists Eric Fulford and Ann Reed. On-site development of the memorial began in late 1998 and concluded with its dedication on Memorial Day in 1999, the last Memorial Day of the millennium. Ninety-five Medal of Honor recipients and a crowd of fifteen thousand spectators were on hand for the event, while another ten million people watched the ceremony on television.

Set on the north bank of the canal in White River State Park, the memorial is an arrangement of twenty-seven curved glass walls, ranging from seven to ten feet tall, representing fifteen conflicts dating back to the Civil War. The names of 3,459 Medal of Honor recipients are etched into the glass. The tribute includes elaborate lighting set to an audio tour; a touch-screen monitor providing visitors with access to additional information on medal recipients and the Medal of Honor itself; and audio recordings, played daily at dusk, of medal honorees recounting their stories of courage and heroism.

Part V

ALL WELCOME PLACES

HISTORIC DESIGNATIONS

There are lots of picture-perfect settings in Indianapolis, but our monuments and memorials remain, year in and year out, the most frequently photographed. They are, hands down, the city's background for everything from family reunions and visitor selfies to travel literature, local TV weather forecasts and national sporting event broadcasts. They are absolutely part of the city "brand," but Indy's trail of memorials are valued well beyond their use as backdrops in photo ops.

They are recognized nationally, not just because the American Legion is headquartered in Indianapolis, but because they were sculpted with rare skill, rarer yet today, and constructed with the finest materials available anywhere in the world. The Indiana War Memorial, in particular, is held up by the nation's top architects as a marvel. And when they are asked, almost as a matter of course, what it might cost to build such a thing today, the answer, invariably, is either that the cost is inestimable or that the work would be an impossible undertaking.

Indy's memorials have been credentialed more officially, too. What was once known as the Indiana World War Memorial Plaza—the four blocks containing American Legion Mall, Veterans Memorial Plaza and the Indiana World War Memorial—was entered in the National Register of Historic Places in 1989, an honor placing the properties among national, state and local sites of significance in our nation's historic, architectural and cultural heritage.

The Historic Memorial District of Downtown Indianapolis

In 1994, the plaza was expanded to include the Marion County Library, just north of the American Legion Mall, and University Park, to the south of the Indiana World War Memorial. At that time, the plaza was renamed the Indiana World War Memorial Plaza Historic District and designated a National Historic Landmark, an even more distinguished honor identifying it as a place of national significance and a noted illustration of American history and heritage.

Finally, in 2016, the Indiana World War Memorial Plaza Historic District was nominated for an expansion of the boundaries to include the Federal Building, south of University Park, and the Soldiers and Sailors Monument on the circle, a block away from the southern edge of the plaza. And because the properties of the historic area were no longer contiguous on the south end, it was renamed the Indiana War Memorials Historic District.

GATHERING PLACES

It is, of course, ironic that the central purpose of war memorials is to remind us very conspicuously of things most of us prefer not to remember or think about. By nature and design, they can be seen as cold and dark places, so it's also a little contradictory that they tend to be the venues of choice for some of a city's biggest celebrations and happiest moments.

Indy's big Downtown Freedom Fest is held every Fourth of July on the grounds of Indiana War Memorial, where some 100,000 people gather to enjoy picnics, live concerts and festive fireworks displays. The Indianapolis 500 Parade, perennially one of the largest and most acclaimed parades in the nation, with attendance usually weighing in at about 250,000, has its brightest moments marching past the memorials. Monument Circle hosts a Strawberry Festival every summer, and the Soldiers and Sailors Monument is transformed into a giant Christmas tree every year in late November as part of the city's traditional Circle of Lights celebration to kick off the holidays.

The circle and the memorial grounds also serve as natural gathering spots for public-service opportunities like safety awareness programs, health and wellness fairs, the Indianapolis Public Schools' Back to School Festival and assemblies of the city's faith communities. They are places of choice for exercising our hard-earned right to voice our opinions and express our differences. They host and encourage the arts and culture with free concerts, walking tours, art fairs, book signings and sporting exhibitions.

The Historic Memorial District of Downtown Indianapolis

But the calendar for the Indiana War Memorials is also full of exactly the kind of celebrations you would expect in such places: Labor Day picnics, Flag Day celebrations and the solemn services that help us appreciate the work of our military and recognize the sacrifices of our veterans and war heroes, including the nation's POWs and MIAs. That's the core work representing the greatest and most essential value of those historic properties.

VISITOR INFORMATION

The Indiana War Memorials are places of history, culture and education. They are parks and open landscapes in the middle of busy city life. Inside and out, they are venues open to public and private gatherings that embrace the spirit of honor and service that is found there.

The Soldiers and Sailors Monument
Originally designed specifically to honor Indiana's Civil War veterans, the Soldiers and Sailors Monument now commemorates the valor of Hoosier veterans of all conflicts prior to World War I. It stands alone as the single most visible symbol of Indianapolis and an icon representing perfectly the establishment of the "Circle City."

A simple, thoughtful walk along the brick-paved circle sidewalk or the base of the monument can in itself be a tribute to Indiana's fallen soldiers. Ambitious visitors are invited to climb the monument's iron staircase of 331 steps or board an elevator for all but the final 31 steps to reach a glass-enclosed observation deck 275 feet above street level. The reward is a beautiful view of the city skyline and the Mile Square in all directions.

The monument is open Wednesdays through Sundays from May to October and Fridays through Sundays from November to April. Hours are 10:30 a.m. to 5:30 p.m. The gathering places on the circle grounds outside the monument are open to the public from dawn to dusk year-round.

The Historic Memorial District of Downtown Indianapolis

The Indiana War Memorial

The Indiana World War Memorial is respected worldwide as a magnificent shrine to global sacrifice and cooperation in the pursuit of freedom. And while it was built specifically to honor veterans of World War I, it now also honors those who have served in more recent conflicts. Visitors stepping into the building for the first time are invariably surprised by the beauty and grandeur of the place, and they walk away with a renewed sense of patriotism. Photos and descriptions of the architecture and the character of the main floor and the Shrine Room can't begin to tell the complete story.

Indoor venues and meeting spaces available to the public include the five-hundred-seat Pershing Auditorium, the Woodfill Boardroom, Spruance and Shoup Halls, the Grand Lobby and the West Foyer. Outdoor spaces on the grounds can accommodate anything from small private groups to larger public events. Gatherings welcome on the grounds of the war memorials include weddings and receptions, festivals, concerts, award ceremonies, meetings, news briefings, conferences and other special events.

But it isn't just about the facilities or the places to see; it's about service. The Indiana War Memorials Commission fills speaking engagements on a wide range of topics for a wide range of audiences. It conducts personal tours, provides self-guided tours, engages home-school families and children with special needs, revitalizes its museum exhibits constantly and provides educational programs for schools, military service organizations and private not-for-profit groups. The commission conducts some 450 programs on the property each year.

The interior of the memorial, including the Shrine Room and the Military Museum on the lower level, are open to the public Wednesdays through Sundays, 9:00 a.m. to 5:00 p.m., and there is no charge for admission. The memorial is closed on all national and state holidays except Memorial Day and Veterans Day. Visitors enter through the main entrance at 55 East Michigan Street, the north side of the building. Reservations are required for use of all Indiana World War Memorial venues. Contact the events coordinator at 317-233-0529 or events@iwm.in.gov to check availability, to schedule a tour of a venue or to request additional information.

The American Legion Headquarters

The American Legion National Headquarters building on Meridian Street, which became the home of the Indiana American Legion, enjoys a rich legacy. In addition to serving as the American Legion's first permanent home, it was the building in which the Legion drafted documents that led to the G.I. Bill and the modern Department of Veterans Affairs. But in recent years, the Indiana American Legion has found that the expense of maintaining the old building has grown beyond what its budget allows, and it has relocated to new offices at Fort Benjamin Harrison on the city's northeast side.

The Indiana War Memorials Commission, however, remains committed to properly maintaining the original American Legion building and ensuring that it will always be used in a manner consistent with its historical nature and its place on the war memorial property. In February 2020, the building began hosting representatives of every benefit program available to service members, other support programs for veterans, the offices of the Indiana Department of Veterans Affairs and the Hoosier Assistance Foundation. It has been said that this is now the only facility in the country offering all of these benefits under one roof.

The National Legion building along Pennsylvania Street continues to serve as the group's national headquarters, and the American Legion remains the nation's largest organization of veterans. Indianapolis is home base to an American Legion family of more than three million members and nearly thirteen thousand posts located throughout the United States and other countries worldwide. And it's fitting that the Legion is located in a state where citizens continue to serve in the military at disproportionately high rates. Even now, for example, Indiana is the sixteenth most populous state but has the fourth-largest National Guard.

The Legion also continues to encourage new membership: "Anyone who has served federal active duty in the United States Armed Forces since December 7, 1941, and has been honorably discharged or is still serving is eligible for membership in The American Legion."

Guided tours of the interior of the American Legion National Headquarters and, in particular, the fourth-floor museum, Fine Arts Gallery and NEC Room, are available by visiting the information desk located inside the Pennsylvania Street entrance. Hours are Mondays through Fridays, 8:30 a.m. to 4:00 p.m.

The Outdoor Memorials
University Park is the oldest part of the Indiana War Memorials Historic District. It has remained a place for city dwellers and city workers alike to "rest and restore" since the state legislature handed jurisdiction of the park over to the Indianapolis Board of Park Commissioners in 1895. And it continues to bear the distinct imprint of George Kessler's redesign in 1914.

The Historic Memorial District of Downtown Indianapolis

Veterans Memorial Plaza is one of the most popular gathering spaces for the city's civic events and, in particular, for the celebration of our nation's national holidays. When it was last reconfigured in 2005, Veterans Memorial Plaza was rededicated as "a perpetual honor to all members of the armed forces of the United States of America in times of war and peace."

Like Veterans Memorial Plaza, the American Legion Mall has long been a popular urban setting for community celebrations. But its perimeter of tributes—the World War II Memorial, the Vietnam War Memorial, the Korean War Memorial and Cenotaph Square—surrounding the mall's sunken garden call for visits and uses of the space that are particularly mindful of our fallen Hoosiers.

The Canal Walk memorials are not so much gathering places as they are beautiful landmarks at which to stop and reflect. The USS *Indianapolis* CA35 Memorial, the Congressional Medal of Honor National Memorial and the Indiana 9/11 State Memorial offer visitors an opportunity to honor our war heroes from the path of the beautiful Central Canal. They are also within easy walking distance of recreational facilities like White River State Park; Victory Field, home of the Indianapolis Indians; and Lucas Oil Stadium, home of the Indianapolis Colts. Memorials located near foot traffic help families engage more conveniently and more naturally with Indy's military history.

University Park, Veterans Memorial Plaza, the American Legion Mall and the three memorials along the Central Canal are all open to the public every day from dawn to dusk free of charge.

A NOBLE PURPOSE

It seems important to conclude with a clear-eyed acknowledgement of the challenges of the past and the present. Every citizen of Indianapolis is connected in some way to the decision made one hundred years ago to build the state's war memorials here. We're all part of it, but the construction of any civic memorial is almost always an imperfect proposition. They are costly to build and maintain. They aren't always seen as representing the best use of public funds. They come with opportunity costs that can include support for important social programs. And not everyone, necessarily, finds them to be aesthetically pleasing contributions to the cityscape.

Brigadier General J. Stewart Goodwin, longtime executive director of the Indiana War Memorials Commission, and his staff, also openly acknowledge a certain level of public apathy toward the memorial properties. "Just about every day, we hear a visitor comment that they have lived in the Indianapolis area for decades and have never been inside our museum. We feel we're the best-kept secret in the state, and we work every day for that not to be the case."

In some cases, war memorials are also associated with feelings of regret over the historical, or potentially historical, structures they displaced. Change, of course, can be very difficult, and there is grief in the process. For some, there is no denying the lasting sadness of losing beautiful old buildings, but it should also be noted that many of the organizations occupying structures in the footprint of the Indiana War Memorials— the Indiana School for the Blind, the Second Presbyterian Church and the First Baptist Church being notable examples—ultimately acquitted themselves very well in moves to larger, modern structures and campuses far more suitable to their emerging needs.

In Indianapolis, the Indiana War Memorials Commission is always focused squarely on a singular purpose, and the mission doesn't change: "To commemorate the valor, honor, and sacrifice of those Hoosier Service Members who served their State and Nation, and to never forget those who paid the ultimate sacrifice." General Goodwin had no trouble describing *his* particular vision for the future of the memorial grounds: to *continue* to do those things. One of his favorite quotes is from President Calvin Coolidge: "The nation which forgets its defenders will itself be forgotten."

It's a lofty cause that begins with the earthly work of keeping the properties in good shape, work that starts early and never ends. A renovation of the Soldiers and Sailors Monument is planned in 2020 to waterproof the basement and repair the walking surfaces. The Indiana War Memorial building itself began to require repairs to the exterior before the building was complete. Its structural needs are unique, and the inevitable repairs are expensive. A multimillion-dollar facelift in 1995, for example, included refurbishing *Pro Patria*, adding accommodations to bring the building up to ADA standards, updating the heating and cooling systems and undertaking a new round of major work to halt erosion of the building's exterior. And in 2018, work began on costly repairs to a leaking roof. Its exotic ziggurat, the pyramidal stepped tower with its wide horizontal surfaces, worked well in arid Mesopotamia, but it presents certain challenges under the snow and rain of central Indiana. The bill for the fix to the roof was roughly equal to the cost of building the memorial in 1926. Over time and on balance, the memorial has been maintained beautifully and has held up, despite the considerable obstacles.

The stewards of the memorials also face property management needs that are less predictable and yet equally unavoidable. There is little anyone can do to fully protect public property from theft or vandalism. Small sculptures have disappeared from University Park on more than one occasion, and in more recent years, thieves stole a ninety-two-year-old pewter plaque dedicating the park's Depew Memorial Fountain. It goes with the territory. And at every turn, there is the possibility of controversy and disagreement. In a nearly one-hundred-year history, there could be no avoiding an occasional fund shortage or a period in which a memorial has fallen into some disrepair. And there is no chance that a concerned citizen will not be critical at some point of how the properties are being managed or utilized. Memorials seem built to invite scrutiny—and they should be scrutinized.

Despite the setbacks and the operational challenges that inevitably come with the mission, the commission, in partnership with groups such as the American Legion, Veterans of Foreign Wars and Disabled American Veterans, continues to work hard to make the properties of the Indiana War Memorials Historic District as beautiful, active, respectful and engaging as they can be. They are also grateful for the generosity of their financial supporters, most notably the State of Indiana, Lily Endowment, the Indiana War Memorials Foundation and an army of private citizens who are also avid students of history.

The commission and its partners always welcome new educational programs, new artists and free public events to the grounds of the memorials. Those things bring culture and the arts to the heart of the city. They are at work finding innovative ways—new technology in audio, video and lighting—to tell young people real and relevant stories about Hoosier heroes and Indiana's storied military history. In late 2019, Downtown Indy Inc. and the Indiana War Memorials Commission premiered the "Shining a Light" program, which transformed Monument Circle into an outdoor theater featuring nightly video and light shows starring Indiana veterans, active-duty soldiers and images reflecting American patriotism. But more than anything else, the partners behind the memorials of downtown Indianapolis are about finding ways to bring the history to life for more than an afternoon or a single event, and all without turning away from the dignity and the reverence the memorials deserve.

Indianapolis has in recent years drawn a new wave of venturous young citizens to its downtown. Bright new apartments and condominiums are part of the growing skyline, and right alongside sits the contrasting memorial district. But it shouldn't be considered the dark side or the relic of the Mile Square; it's the history and the heritage holding its place in the center of everything else the city has become. It's a good reflection of us and a noble use of the land. Those pieces of granite and limestone that stand there can, at once, be both beautiful and sobering—works of art that also help us remember those who have made a good life in the big city a possibility to begin with.

BIBLIOGRAPHY

Books

Barrows, Robert G., and David J. Bodenhamer. *The Encyclopedia of Indianapolis*. Bloomington: Indiana University Press, 1994, 23, 30, 31, 254, 255, 746, 762, 763, 804, 1121, 1164, 1224, 1233, 1278, 1279, 1375.

Harris, Bill. *Indianapolis: An Illustrated History*. San Marcos, CA: Heritage Media, 2004.

Indianapolis Architecture: Transformations Since 1975. Indianapolis: Indiana Architectural Foundation, 1993.

Indianapolis City Directory Guide. Indianapolis, IN: Indianapolis Journal Company, 1855, first issue.

Madden, W.C. *Indianapolis in Vintage Postcards*. Charleston, SC: Arcadia Publishing, 2003.

———. *Indianapolis: Then & Now*. Charleston, SC: Arcadia Publishing, 2003, 83, 84, 203.

Rose, Ernestine Bradford. *The Circle: The Center of Our Universe*. Indianapolis: Indiana Historical Society, 1957.

Tenuth, Jeffrey. *Indianapolis: A Circle City History*. Charleston, SC: Arcadia Press, 2004, 23–31.

BIBLIOGRAPHY

Brochures and Pamphlets

American Legion. *American Legion National Headquarters, Emil A. Blackmore Museum.* Indianapolis, Indiana.
———. *American Legion National Headquarters, Indianapolis, IN, A Tour Guide for 94th National Convention of the American Legion.* Indianapolis, Indiana.
———. *American Legion National Headquarters Tour Guide.* Indianapolis, Indiana.
Congressional Medal of Honor Memorial. Indianapolis, Indiana.
Finneran, Patrick J. *The USS Indianapolis CA-35 National Memorial.* Indianapolis, Indiana, 1996.
Indiana State Library. *Indiana State Soldiers and Sailors Monument.* Indianapolis, Indiana, 1900.
———. *The Indiana World War Memorial.* Indianapolis, Indiana.
Indiana War Memorials Commission. *American Legion Mall.* Indianapolis, Indiana.
———. *The Indiana War Memorials.* R-04/14. Indianapolis, Indiana.
———. *Indiana War Memorials Commission Pocket Guide.* Indianapolis, Indiana.
———. *Indiana World War I—Centennial Committee.* Indianapolis, Indiana.
———. *Indiana World War Memorial and Veteran's Memorial Plaza.* Indianapolis, Indiana.
———. *Soldiers and Sailors Monument, Indianapolis, Indiana.* Indianapolis, Indiana.

Newspapers and Magazines

Howard, William Willard. "The City of Indianapolis." Supplement to *Harper's Weekly*, August 11, 1888.
Indianapolis Business Journal, June 8, 2018.
Indianapolis Daily Journal, April 1, 1862.
Indianapolis News, July 30, 1919; November 11, 1919; September 14, 1923; February 24, 1926; November 6, 1926; November 27, 1926; April 28, 1928, August 2, 1930; November 15, 1930; March 11, 1937; March 31, 1937; March 15, 1939; May 11, 1939; February 21, 1945; June 19, 1966; March 20, 1969.
Indianapolis Star, May 7, 1922; July 8, 1923; October 23, 1930; June 21, 1931; April 7, 1935; November 14, 1935; May 30, 1939; September 23, 1943; February 16, 1945; July 1, 1956; July 29, 1959; July 8, 1962; June 19, 1966; July 11, 1971; August 11, 1983; July 3, 1996; November 23, 1996;

June 13, 1999; March 13, 2009; February 9, 2018; February 19, 2018; October 28, 2018; November 8, 2018, December 9, 2018.
Indianapolis Times, March 31, 1937; May 3, 1944; May 5, 1944; July 4, 1945.
Noland, Stephen, C. "Indiana's War Memorial." *National Republic* 15, no. 5 (September 1927).
Perry Township Weekly. "Bob Dole to Keynote World War II Memorial Dedication in Indianapolis." April 16, 1998.
Shield. "Indiana's World War Memorial." July–September 1927.

Internet Sources

"American Legion History." www.newspapers.com.
Baist Real Estate Atlas Collection. IUPUI University Library. www.ulib.iupuidigital.org.
Bilger, Nathan. "Preservation Denied: Blind Institute." Posted May 20, 2011. www.historicindianapolis.com.
Browne, Tiffany Benedict. "Then & Now: At Vermont and Meridian, Parts I and II." Posted January 16, 2019 and January 30, 2019. www.historicindianapolis.com.
Cierzniak, Libby. "Indianapolis Collected: The North-South Battle Over University Square." Posted May 26, 2012. www.historicindianapolis.com.
"Depew Memorial Fountain—Indianapolis, Indiana." Smithsonian Art Inventory Sculptures. www.waymarking.com.
"Explore—Indiana War Memorials." Indiana War Memorials. www.indianawarmemorials.org.
General Information about Indiana War Memorials. Indiana State Government. www.in.gov/iwm.
"General John Morgan and His Raiders Invade Indiana." 1863 Civil War Journey. Conner Prairie. www.connerprairie.org.
History of American Wars. https://www.gettysburgflag.com.
Hostetler, Joan. "Then & Now: Indiana Democratic Club." Posted August 30, 2012. www.historicindianapolis.com.
———. "Then & Now: Second Presbyterian Church and World War Memorial." Posted July 25, 2013. www.historicindianapolis.com.
"Indiana Legion to Vacate Historic Meridian Street Building." March 14, 2014. www.ibj.com.

BIBLIOGRAPHY

Indianapolis City Directory. A.C. Grooms and W.T. Smith. IUPUI University Library. www.ulib.iupuidigital.org.

Indianapolis City Directory. R.L. Polk & Co. IUPUI University Library. ulib.iupuidigital.org.

Landscapes and Architecture. The Cultural Landscape Foundation. tclf.org.

"Mausoleum at Halicarnassus." Ancient History Encyclopedia. www.ancient.eu/Mausoleum_at_Halicarnassus.

Official Tourism Site of Indianapolis, Indiana War Memorial Properties. www.visitindy.com.

"Public Space Information." Indiana War Memorials. www.downtownindy.org.

Ryan, Jordan. "Flats Lost: Memorial Plaza." Posted December 1, 2012. www.historicindianapolis.com.

Sanborn Fire Insurance Maps. IUPUI University Library. www.ulib.iupuidigital.org.

"Tinian Island." Atomic Heritage Foundation. www.atomicheritage.org/location/tinian-island.

"The Worst Naval Disaster in US History." USS Indianapolis CA-35. www.ussindianapolis.org.

Documents

The Indiana World War Memorial. State of Indiana Documents. Indiana State Library.

Report of the Indiana World War Memorial Study Commission. Indiana State Library, November 1, 1954.

ABOUT THE AUTHOR

Rudy Schouten is a freelance commercial writer focused on developing sales material and marketing content but enjoys projects on the side writing nonfiction of a less business-like nature. *The Historic Memorial District of Downtown Indianapolis* is the result of his personal interest in the history and the evolution of the city and its landmarks, much of it within walking distance of his upbringing on the near north side. Fueled by the still clear images he has collected along the way, the book reflects his curiosity over how much downtown Indianapolis has changed, and how much it hasn't. Rudy and his wife, Cindy, live on Indy's south side.

Visit us at
www.historypress.com

www.ingramcontent.com/pod-product-compliance
Lightning Source LLC
Chambersburg PA
CBHW042140160426
43201CB00021B/2352